In this haunting and stunnin̲ Somehow, she tells us a story t̲ Somehow, she manages to tell Joe's bold and painful story while her own story simultaneously sneaks in. With breathtaking grace, Benedix navigates the wild, wandering shapes that such stories can take on. And because she invites her readers in so graciously, we are not merely on-lookers or voyeurs. Benedix offers us the chance to become active agents in the storytelling. She allows us to become empathy detectives. And so Benedix tells us Joe's story, and her story, and even our own.

Sarah Gerkensmeyer, Author of *what you are now enjoying,* winner of the Autumn House Fiction Prize, Late Night Library's Debut-litzer, and the Indiana Authors Award

Some writers know that every life story takes form within the constraints of genre, the expectations of readers, the stubborn reality of their subject, and the stubborn integrity of the author herself driven to convey a fullest possible truth. Within the arena of books about Holocaust survivors, only a very few authors have had the knowledge, talent, and commitment to describe that quest in detail. In this vitally important book, Beth Benedix shows herself to be one of those very few. Beautifully conveyed, informed and informing, Benedix shows us what it means to listen to a Holocaust survivor—and to listen to our own listening—with unflinching integrity, candor, and care. This book asks the right questions and—almost unique in writing about survivors—it grounds those questions within the complexity of a full relationship. Benedix cherishes that complexity because she knows it is the real, irreducible thing.

Hank Greenspan, author of *On Listening to Holocaust Survivors, Reflections: Auschwitz, Memory and a Life* and the acclaimed play, "Remnants."

Ghost Writer

A Story About Telling a Holocaust Story

Beth Benedix

SPUYTEN DUYVIL
NEW YORK CITY

Library of Congress Cataloging-in-Publication Data

Names: Hawkins Benedix, Beth, 1971- author. | Koenig, Joe (Joseph), 1927-
author.
Title: Ghost writer : a story about telling a Holocaust story / Beth Benedix.
Description: New York City : Spuyten Duyvil, [2018]
Identifiers: LCCN 2017044320 | ISBN 9781947980013 (pbk.)
Subjects: LCSH: Koenig, Joe (Joseph), 1927- | Hawkins Benedix, Beth, 1971- |
Jews--Poland-- Częstochowa--Biography. | Holocaust, Jewish
(1939-1945)--Poland--Częstochowa --Personal narratives. | Częstochowa
(Poland)--Biography. | Authorship--Collaboration. | Narration (Rhetoric)
Classification: LCC DS134.72.K63 H39 2018 | DDC 940.53/18092 [B] --dc23
LC record available at https://lccn.loc.gov/2017044320

For Joe

" So what time of day was it? What color was the sky? What was I wearing? What was I thinking about? What was the date?"

Joe was teasing me—gently—for asking so many questions. I wanted scenes, I told him, *needed* scenes and details to set the stage for our readers. A few weeks before our first meeting, I had emailed Joe a numbered list of what seemed to me to be particularly graphic moments in his story, with instructions to remember as many details as possible about these moments and to relate them to me the next time we met.

Right then, we were tackling Question #6 on my list:

Can you set the scene when you were hiding in the cornfield in the outskirts of Czestochowa? What were you thinking? Was it sunny? Grey? Cold? Hot? How long were you sitting there holding your breath?

Our meeting place—a glassed-in boardroom in Joe's son's investment firm on the 64th floor of a corporate building on Chicago's Wacker Drive—was cold. Really cold. Whenever I started to shiver, Joe grabbed my hands between his own, rubbing them together like he was teaching me how to start a fire with a stick.

"You're so cold, baby!" he would say.

"I'm okay," I reassured him.

But I pulled my coat on after the first warm-up, and pulled it tighter around me throughout the afternoon. My throat was raw by the time the train deposited me back home that night. The room seemed all sharp edges, even if the sprawling ebony table—built to accommodate ten, fifteen people—was round. No human flourishes, no traces of color or whimsy, it was a room meant for brokering deals. Joe and I sat next to each other on wheeled leather chairs at the far end, our backs turned on the expansive view of Lake Michigan stretching out from the window behind us.

"Readers are going to want to *see* all of this, Joe," I pestered. "They won't believe what you went through."

"Won't believe it? *Won't believe me?* Let me ask you something. Do you believe me?"

He looked me straight in the eye, his mouth clamped shut.

"Of course I do. That's not what I meant. I didn't mean that they wouldn't *believe* you, but that your story is amazing. It's just amazing that you were able to make it through so much."

I repeated the series of questions that made up Question #6, hell-bent on getting answers.

"I mean… what were you *thinking* about in that cornfield?" I asked. "How long were you sitting there holding your breath, knowing that they were just one row over?"

"Amazing? No. I just did what I had to do. You know? I just did it. That's just how it is, you know. You want all these details, but that's not important. Was it afternoon? Was it evening? Was I cold? Was I hot?" He motioned his hand back and forth, brushing aside the silliness of it all.

"Listen to me, okay? Basically, you're asking me what I thought. That I was almost dead, right? Am I right or wrong? Well this is very simple: I tell you what, when you have someone a few steps next to you or on the other side of you and you know this man or lady is here to kill you, okay, you do everything possible to stop and think what to do. Nothing else is on your mind except 'how do I get out of this situation alive?' I'm not thinking, 'is it cold? Is it gray?' The weather's got nothing to do with it! *Because I can't make a move.* They were on my ass. All you have to do is keep your breath and hope that you will get away as soon as possible. Nothing else matters except to get out of this cornfield knowing that your enemy is waiting for you. You see what I mean?"

This was our dance, our back and forth, our routine, how we went about negotiating our own deal in this boardroom. Ever-eager for a seamless narrative, I would prompt Joe for details that could cohere into the perfect arc. I was looking for beginnings, middles, and ends, for a linear story that could then be deconstructed, analyzed, and mined for its symbolic potential. Joe's accompanying move was to sidestep in an elegant, but firm, dismissal of the importance of these details and a reassertion of the ground beneath us. And to insist that only one question really matters in a story of survival: *How do I get out of this situation alive?*

Symbolism and a wish for seamless narrative, it turns out, have precious little to do with that question. But I didn't yet know how little I knew about all that. Or about how far a story of survival can extend.

PART ONE: MEETING JOE

Here's how it started.

In the fall of 2008, my colleague, Peter, asked me if I might be interested in working with a Holocaust survivor, Joe Koenig, and his family to tell his story. "I'll give you the number if you are," he told me. Peter's neighbor, it turned out, worked for Joe's daughter, and she was putting out feelers for someone who could pick up the pieces of what had been several prior attempts by others to write Joe's story.

I teach at DePauw University, in Greencastle Indiana, about 4 hours from Skokie, IL, Joe's home. Bit of a distance, it seemed to me, to go to solicit a ghostwriter, if that's what the gig was intended to be. But there it was, an offer out of the blue, a throwaway question that could easily have been thrown away. It wasn't exactly convenient to take on a project like this: I was teaching full time, acclimating to two-kid motherhood (two sons with less than two years between them), and sleep deprived from nursing my 1 ½ year old all night (attachment issues on both sides).

Peter's question made sense, from an academic perspective. While we have a bona fide Holocaust historian at DePauw, I was the go-to person for Holocaust literature. Or rather, I was the person people tended to go to about literature that grows out of the Holocaust, and that juts up against it, darkly prescient. Existentialism to the nth degree. Fiction. Poetry. Drama. Philosophy. Modern Jewish literature. Kafka. Nietzsche. This was the stuff I taught and wrote about. The stuff I thought endlessly about. The stuff I tortured one of my graduate school professors with. "Beth," she said once, thoroughly exasperated, in the middle of a seminar, "you have to stop approaching *all* German literature from *all* time as if leads directly to the Holocaust." (Point taken, but misplaced; we were reading a Wagnerian libretto.)

Though it's hard to pinpoint, I'm pretty sure my obsession with the Holocaust started the night I was forced to watch "Night and Fog" in Hebrew school when I was about eleven. I had no frame of reference then—and still don't—for how to process the grainy images of dead bodies piled on one another, or of emaciated live bodies with too-large-seeming heads, rib-bones piercing skin. But the images implanted themselves, and I live with them. In particular, I'm haunted by one image, when the camera takes us into a men's bunk in Auschwitz. The men are crowded into the bunks, some sitting on the edges, chests concave, others lying on their backs or bellies. In my memory, the men are all looking into the camera. It's their eyes that haunt me—how human they still remain—and the range of responses in them: disbelief, despair, anger, fear, amusement (on some of the men's faces, I seem to remember, are traces of a grin or full-fledged smiles). I have spent the better part of my professional career trying to make sense of how eyes can continue to look so human in the midst of such a profound void of humanity.

When Peter asked me if I was interested, I was looking for a new project. I'd just sent out the proofs for an edited collection of essays on subversive uses of the Bible in modern literature[1] and recently shelved a project that was going nowhere: a case study of my dad, who died in 1992, when I was twenty. "Prodigal Father," I was calling it. The epigraph came from Kafka, a line from his short story, "The Judgment": "my father is still a giant of a man." The spirit—but, alas, none of the subtlety—of Kafka's "Letter to His Father" loomed over the thing, rendering it part lament, part accusation. I wanted to find out what made him "tick," this man who had thumbed his nose at the basic rules of society.

Good timing though it was, it *scared* me to think about working with Joe. It took me far out of my comfort zone, which was the world of ideas. Set me up with an obscure poem or enigmatic Kafka parable, and I can do a mean literary analysis. Need a gloss on covenantal theology and its ethical implications? I'm your girl. Existential musings on the nature of memory and how we memorialize? Check. But what did I know about this feet-all-too-firmly-planted-on-the-ground kind of writing, about writing with such high stakes? I'd never written anything like this before. At that point, my idea of academic risk-taking was to write in the first person. Boldness is relative.

And, too, there's the fact that my default mode tends towards near-pathological shyness when it comes to meeting new people and that the idea of calling a stranger sends me into phobic fits. Mousy, I think, might be a word some people would use to describe me when they first meet me. It doesn't last long, though, that first impression.

The shyness generally dissolves quickly into gushiness and a constitutional inability to not say what I'm thinking. I am a person who wears her heart perpetually on her sleeve, a worse poker player you'll never meet. I recognize that it's a strange and not altogether consistent set of traits to exist together—the way I teeter between nose-in-book and tell-all-feel-all. It catches some people off guard. It catches *me* off guard sometimes.

But, despite all that, I was interested. The chance to help a Holocaust survivor tell his story, to confront the brutal reality of the literature I had lived in for so long, to break away from the stilted and lifeless writing I felt somehow condemned to produce—that was more appealing to me than I could articulate, even to myself. I wanted to know who this man was and how he could have lived through all that he had lived through. And I knew that time was running out—for me and everyone else—to hear these first person accounts. In ten or fifteen years, there will be no one left to tell his or her own story.

"Yes!" I told Peter. "Thank you so much for thinking of me."

*

Two days later, white-knuckling the phone, I called the number Peter gave me. It was Joe's son's.

Unnerved as I was by the vetting process, it was a nice conversation. We spoke about my credentials and what the family was looking for from the process. He told me about the other women the family had hired[2] prior to me, and how their drafts, which he said he would send to me,[3] did not meet their expectations. "We want it to read more like a story," he told me. "Not so cut-and-dried. The other versions are more like facts strung together, more like stream-of-consciousness. We want to have a narrative for the family that puts it all together." He asked if I would send him a copy of my first book (which casts Kafka, and two, more obscure, poets, Paul Celan and Edmond Jabès, as "reluctant theologians")[4] to share with his siblings, so that they could get a sense of my writing style. I did, my last copy, though it felt a little like a bait and switch, in that I had already vowed to myself never to write that kind of ethereal nonsense again.

It nagged at me a little bit that he seemed to have no qualms about handing over those other drafts (would the women want me to have them?).[5] It felt as though I was headed into murky territory. I couldn't quite put my finger on it. The lingering trace of that failed dad-project, the meeting of a Holocaust survivor in flesh-and-blood, the palpable sense that I was closing one door and opening another. The not-knowing what might be behind that door.

I chalked it up to basic cowardice.

Two weeks after talking with Joe's son, having closely read and marked up those prior drafts he had sent me, I made the trek with my husband and two sons to Joe's daughter's impeccable townhouse in Chicago, to hammer out the details of how and when I would set about the project of writing this man's larger-than-life life. Joe and his whole family were there: three sons, daughter and wife. Given my stranger-anxiety, I was totally out of my element. I felt inadequate. Frumpy. Bumbling. Greencastle is a far cry from downtown Chicago.

But Joe came right up to me, touched my cheek and smiled mischievously. "So you want to do this thing, eh? You really want to do it?"

With him, immediately, I felt at home. This man, standing stoop-shouldered next to me, barely a few inches taller than my own 5'1" frame, rocking ever-so-slightly on his feet, alternately tugging the sleeve-bottoms of his black-flecked sweater mid-palm with his fingertips and jamming his hands in the pockets of his tan corduroys, wire-framed glasses poised in front of muddy brown eyes and thinning brows, wispy shock of gray-brown hair combed back tightly from his creased and spotted forehead, heavy Polish accent draped over the lilting cadence of his voice—he felt familiar, familial. I had to resist the urge to hug him, to keep up professional appearances. Those appearances still meant something to me at the time.

Remnants of a brunch between us, my husband and two sons having been dispatched to a nearby playground (there were too many breakables—colorful *tchotchkes*, Faberge eggs and porcelain nesting dolls and Russian pottery, perched invitingly on the glass coffee table—to leave it up to chance), we got down to business. One of Joe's sons handed me a glossy-covered, off-sized paperback. A self-published Holocaust memoir.

"This is the kind of thing we're looking for, Beth. Do you think you could write something like this, with those drafts you have?"

I flipped through the pages, wanting to be polite, but my heart sank a little. This book somehow felt too small, too confining, for Joe. The man I had encountered in the multiple drafts his son had given me seemed—already in this first meeting—to swell beyond any book I'd read before.

Ever-afraid of conflict, I smiled and acknowledged to them what I believed it must have taken for the author to have written the book they'd just handed me, how painful the process must have been, how necessary for her family that she preserve her story in this concrete object that they could hold in their hands.

"It's a beautiful-looking book and I have a better sense now of what you're asking of me. But here's kind of what I'm thinking," I said tentatively. "I don't know yet what shape this book is going to take. I think the shape will only start to present itself after Joe and I have had a chance to really sit down and talk and get to know each other."

I took a breath, fighting with myself, at once trying to muster up the courage to say the thing I was thinking and to stop myself from saying it.

"But here's the thing." I decided to go for it. "I know this sounds really crass, and I'm sorry if it comes across as insensitive, but there are just so many Holocaust memoirs out there. There's a glut in the market. If we want to market Joe's story to a wide audience—and I know I do—I feel like I have to find a way to tell his story that hasn't been done before. I feel like Joe's story *deserves* a wide audience, because there's just so much going on here. I want to introduce the world to Joe. People are going to love him!"

I was talking with my hands at this point, gesticulating vigorously as I tend to do when I get nervous or excited. I felt, palpably, the audacity of what I had just said—*marketing Joe's story to a wide audience?* No one had asked me to do this. A brief out-of-body sensation: disbelief at the uncharacteristic nerviness I was displaying. *Where had this person come from all of a sudden?* But I couldn't seem to help myself. I think in universals, grand designs. I wanted them to see the potential largeness of it all.

So I kept going.

"I want people to come away as inspired by Joe as I was when I read those drafts. I don't know, I'm kind of thinking at this point that one approach to the story might be to cast Joe as a philosopher. As I read the drafts, that's what I just kept coming back to. He's a philosopher."

I had been careful to scan the room as I said all this, trying to involve everyone in my thought process. But now I looked across the table at Joe and said directly to him: "Joe, you've got such a totally unique way of looking at things."

He raised his eyebrow, skeptical. We stared at each other, sussing one another out.

I couldn't get past the fact that, in those drafts, Joe seemed to be asking and encouraging others to ask the "big" questions—about life and love and meaning and non-meaning. It seemed to me that he was describing an ethical code, that he had found a way to live his life that had both everything and nothing to do with his experience during the Holocaust. I wanted to figure it out, how he pulled off what seemed to be the impossible feat of staying sane in the midst of and following everything he had gone through. *More* than sane. *Healthy.*

An excruciating silence. Then Joe burst out:

"That's it? That's all you've got? You've read my entire story and that's the best you can come up with? I'm a *philosopher*?"

He looked more amused than upset. Surprised, maybe. The rest of the family said nothing. I thought I caught a glimpse of one son rolling his eyes at another.

Well, that's it, I thought. *It's over. I've lost them.*

I looked down at the slice of tomato on my plate, then back up, grasping for the words to explain what I had meant, how it was that I could have reduced this man who had lost his entire family by the time he was fifteen, who had lived through four camps and two death marches and went on to serve both the Israeli and U.S Armies in wartime, who was forced in every sense of the word to gather his wits and trust his intuition… to a… *philosopher?*

I was pretty sure I was blowing it. Yes, I was blowing it. *What was I thinking, imposing my own sense of project onto this cut-and-dried assignment?* The more I blew it, it became more and more important to me not to. Not out of any sense of professionalism, rapidly dwindling with every second of silence, but because I sensed something infinite, urgent, necessary in my sitting here across from Joe. Something inescapable. It felt as if something had been propelling me towards this moment, towards my meeting Joe.

I tried again, willing the lump that seemed to have just lodged itself in my throat to go away.

"What I mean... it's just that... okay, here it is..." I looked again at Joe. Inhaled the near-chemical smell of exasperation that hung over the table. "Your name. It captures everything for me. *Koenigheit.* Kingliness—nobility. The way it gets shortened to Koenig when you come to the US—I don't know, I'm hung up on the symbolism of it all. I read your story and I think to myself, 'that's it, that's who this guy is. That's what he's all about. That's how he got through all of this.'"

Except that, by the time I got to *got through,* the lump in my throat had morphed into tears that now spilled over my face.

Oh my God, I'm such a loser, I thought, humiliated. Grabbed at napkins to stem the flow of snot and tears. *It's definitely over.*

Joe reached for my hand across the table. Took it. Smiled.

"Okay, kid. Now you listen to me. I'm going to tell you something: You're the tailor, okay? I'm going to give you these pieces, these little pieces. And you need to take those pieces and put them together, like a suit, okay? The story is like a suit."

The second time I met Joe was in his son's boardroom about a month after my crying spell, which, shockingly, hadn't disqualified me from the job.

It was February 2009.

That morning, I had taken the 7:35 train from Crawfordsville, Indiana, to Chicago, set to arrive at Union Station at 11:15 (gaining an hour as we crossed into Central time). I planned to return on the 5:45, giving Joe and me roughly five and a half hours to talk (building in time to get to and from Union Station).

I would take this trip two more times over the next four months, collecting the pieces from Joe that I needed to craft his story. 4-5 hours up, 4-5 hours back, depending on the freight traffic. In the rural hinterlands of central Indiana, passenger trains yield to freights. It is possible (and probable, it turns out) to sit on the tracks for an hour or more while industrial or agricultural materials move on schedule to their destination. It occurred to me more than once on this always-stalled train that gives priority to the inanimate how insignificant the human drama really is.

About an hour into the train ride, snowy fields sliding by my window, I took the glossy paperback out of my computer bag. I turned it over and over, contemplating the grainy picture of the author on the front cover and the blurb—a paragraph detailing the author's "harrowing tale of survival"—on the back. As I looked, the author's picture seemed to fade away, Joe's eighty-one-year-old face superimposing itself over hers. I imagined him grinning at me, shaking his head and saying, *No, not this way. There's another way to tell my story.*

In the intervening weeks between that first meeting and this one, I kept coming back to that paperback, and to the heart-sinking feeling I'd had when his family handed it to me. The feeling had actually taken me by surprise. I was well acquainted with these sorts of memoirs—first-person narratives of survival, often written by an amanuensis, that record, collect, protect, and pass on memory—and had always found them to be both moving and deeply important.

I am a firm believer in the spirit of the mantra *Never forget*, though I would suggest changing it to *Always remember*. It's still a directive, but it shifts the emphasis to the active work, the creative process, of remembering, of making embodied once again. To me, memories are *corporeal*, they have weight and substance and consequences. At some point in my literary studies, I was won over by Freud's insistence that memory-making works as two-part process and product, first as an act of retrieval of raw data (text), second as the scaffolding of that data in meaningful narrative (context). For this reason, I admire Stephen Spielberg, endlessly, for founding the Visual History project,[6] for creating the venue for so many voices to be preserved in their own context. We *need* these testimonies of how grossly humans betrayed one another, these accounts of how it is still possible to survive a system calculated to destroy. We *need* those details that mean something only to the first-person speaker, because it's in those details that history is made human, that the human element destroyed is also retrieved.

It's just that, when Joe's son handed me the book, it hit me that not only did I *not want* to write that kind of book, I didn't feel capable of writing it. I wasn't *that* kind of Holocaust scholar, with all the details of history at her fingertips. Hell, I hadn't even been to see the camps, having concocted an elaborate rationalization of my decision not to do so when I was in Germany. This detail hadn't been outed in my conversation with Joe's son or the brunch with Joe and his family, and I carried it with me with more than a little shame. Somehow, though, coming face to face with my scholarly limitations only drew me more powerfully to Joe and his story. The hallucination—wish-fulfillment though it certainly was, my way of imagining Joe granting me license to ditch a tried-and-true method that his family clearly favored—captured the closeness that I felt to him but couldn't explain. The tried-and-true just didn't feel right when it came to Joe.

Despite these misgivings, I decided then that, whatever alternative approaches I may have sensed possible in those early days of my relationship with Joe, I owed it to Joe and his family to *really try* to write the kind of story that his family was asking me to write. I wanted to give them his story of survival as a concrete thing in the world, a thing they could hold in their hands. I wanted to honor their wishes. I wanted to honor Joe.

Entering the corporate building on Wacker Drive for the first time, I was struck by the mammoth quality of the place. It was a feeling that didn't go away on subsequent visits. In that building, I was dwarfed. In over my head. Out of my realm. This was the world my students often found themselves in for internships and after graduation. I'd ask them for details about their jobs and quickly lose track of what they had told me. It is a world that doesn't make sense to me, a world I feel vaguely prohibited from entering. My world is circumscribed by classrooms, blackboards, meetings, one-on-one conferences with students about papers and projects. Now, I found myself in this building awash in fountains and marble, escalators delivering the weary to a food court swathed in tall palm fronds. A security guard at the front desk asked me which office I was headed to. He called up, gained clearance, and issued me an identification badge. I took the elevator three levels up to Joe's son's office. Behind a nondescript glass door quietly announcing the name of Joe's son's investment firm, there was an empty reception area with a jar of hard candies and a vase of dried flowers. And just beyond that, I saw Joe sitting in the boardroom, his back to me, alone with his thoughts and *The Chicago Tribune*.

As I had the day in his daughter's townhouse, I felt something like a weight lifting the minute I saw him. In the midst of all this pomp and circumstance, Joe's presence comforted me.

"Ah, sweetie, you made it, you made it," he said, looking up with grin when I opened the door. "Was your trip okay? Are you hungry? Do you need to go to the restroom? Do you need some coffee? Come, let me introduce you to Susan, my son's secretary. She's really the one who runs this place. She can get you anything you need."

Greetings and introductions over, we went back to the boardroom, ready to hunker down for the afternoon, to sort through pages and pages of first drafts of his story transcribed by others, to pursue the gaps and silent spaces. So many gaps, so many silent spaces. Before we sat down, Joe motioned me over to the window that traced the entire length of the room. From this height, we looked out over Lake Michigan, at the spectacular view of the city sprawling below us. A city so far removed from Czestochowa, Poland, the city of Joe's birth, the city of his father's death. The window forced our gaze both east and down—life teeming over haphazardly, noisily, in the grid of streets, then abruptly emptying out in the formless expanse of the lake. We stood there silently for a minute, at once entirely removed from and entirely indebted to the world framed by that window.

"Can you believe this view?" Joe asked. "Can you believe this office? This is my son's office, the whole thing. This is all his. Can you believe my son? What a good kid, my son, what a smart guy. All my kids, such good kids... am I right or am I right?"

Pure pride splashed across his face, unapologetic, unmistakable: a father's joy in his children's success, without staking any claims to it. A pang sliced through me, not exactly nostalgia. Maybe it was nostalgia's opposite: I couldn't remember my own father's face ever looking this way. I looked at Joe, at this small—but by no means frail—man who had once lost everything he had. Who had cheated death more times than he could count, and in the most creative ways. Who made the decision daily to live in the present, not the past.

I looked at him. At his off-white sweater and brown corduroys. His slightly stooped shoulders and wire-rimmed glasses. Remembering his "suit" comment, I panicked a little. I wondered if it showed what a terrible seamstress I am, forever pulling threads too tight, bunching up the material, securing buttons with so many wrap-arounds that they jut out rigidly from the shirt behind them, no longer fitting comfortably inside their intended buttonholes. Wearing out metaphors with too-much deliberation.

Joe looked to be a man completely at home in the story he had lived and others wanted him to tell. As our meetings went on, it became clear to me that he was so at home that, sometimes, he glossed right over the details in his telling, reluctant to mine them for deeper meaning, resisting his own reflections. And I, longing for a coherent narrative that I could give his family, for catharsis and epiphany for my own sake, would try to pin those details down, would try to coax meaning and lessons and clarity from them. Little did I know, as I stood with Joe at this window, thinking vaguely of my own father, that my desire for clarity was a defensive tool, a posture I clung to to protect myself from seeing all that was really there, beyond and behind the details.

Joe grinned, put his arm around me, guided me to the table.

"All right, kid," he said. "Let's get cracking."

PART TWO: THE SUIT

The day the Gestapo came to liquidate Czestochowa's little ghetto, Joe wasn't feeling well. His father told him not to go to work, not to waste his strength carting out and sorting through furniture that had once belonged to the Jews who had already been ushered in cattle cars en masse to Treblinka, Joe's mother and two sisters among them. Joe and his father had been assigned to forced labor, the only reason they escaped a similar fate.

"Don't come, Juszo," his father had said when he left for work with the others in the morning. "You'll stay here in the factory and rest. It will be okay." He touched Joe's cheek gently, cupped his chin in his hand. "It will be okay."

Joe listened. But he felt something wrench inside him. Goodbyes could not be taken casually anymore.

A few hours later, German officers drove into Metallurgia, the mammoth foundry on Krotka Street that had been serving as a barracks.

Joe had been resting, and schmoozing a little, with a few others. He wasn't really that sick, just a bit of a stomachache and a headache that tugged at his temples. Now, as he heard the cars roll in, a more profound nausea took over.

The room spun around him, an acrid stench of fear the instantaneous, involuntary and collective response. It provided a kind of cover for him to withdraw quietly to an unoccupied corner of the building. Here he stood for less than a few seconds, then crept along the wall, moving towards the place where he was sure no one would think to look.

As the officers rounded up some 550 people—350 of whom they deported to Treblinka, 200 who were executed that day in the street outside the foundry, in earshot of Joe—Joe slipped out of the barracks and into another building just beyond it.

When he opened the door to Gestapo headquarters, he said a silent prayer.

"Please God, *please*, don't let them see me."

The staircase was just on the other side of the foyer. To his left and right were offices, filled modestly with people working—underlings, mostly, bureaucrats and paper-pushers, but Gestapo all the same. Too busy to notice the fourteen year-old boy who moved quickly past the open doorframes.

He stepped gingerly onto the first stair, testing it for creaks that might give him away. Hearing none, he bolted up one flight of stairs and then another and another. The stairs ended here, and gave way to a room—empty—where he stopped. A storage space, it looked like it hadn't been used for some time. Joe relaxed. Finding a corner that would hide him from the line of vision—if someone were to come unexpectedly through the door—he sat huddled there for hours, intermittently napping and nursing what had become a more persistent ache in his stomach and head. In the empty room, he tried not to hear his own thoughts, tried not to think about how alone he was. Tried not to think or feel at all.

But try as he might, his thoughts kept drifting back to all he had already lost. He and his father had been away at a nearby work camp—his father, who spoke perfect German, was chosen to serve as foreman—when his mother and two sisters were taken away to Treblinka. Rumors of gas chambers circulated through the ghetto, but Joe had no way of knowing for sure that this was the fate they had met. Sitting here, now, he contemplated the possibility that he would never see them again. He tried not to think of all the things he might have said the last time he saw them, had he known it was the last time. Tried not to think about the playful arguments he'd always had with his sisters in the time "before." It hurt him deeply to remember this life, the nurturing home his mother created, filled with love and laughter, awash in the happy din of the radio and phonographs playing—it seemed perpetually—in the background. Theirs had been a typical Jewish home—observant, but not particularly religious. In this cramped closet, Joe remembered the smell of the warm *challah* his mother baked every Friday. When they returned from synagogue, she would light candles in the sparkling silver candlesticks, and Joe's father would say *Kiddush* over the wine. He remembered, with a sharp pang, the makeshift Bar Mitzvah his parents had managed to organize for him, in a neighbor's apartment, just after the war started. There had been no more temples to go to, then, but they had managed to cobble together a minyan to see their son become an adult in the eyes of tradition.

He was an adult now, so it seemed, but he was really still a child. A scared and hungry fourteen year old, huddled and alone in this place he had somehow found to protect him. Before he could stop it from coming, a collapsed moment, the symbol for him of a happier time, came into his thoughts: the bicycle that his father had bought for him, out of the blue on a summer day the year before the Germans had invaded Poland. His father had taken him to the bicycle shop and told him to pick one out. The one he chose was midnight blue, with light-colored, unpainted wooden rims bent forward like rams' horns. A racing bike. Joe rode it everywhere his parents would let him, and, when he returned home, would lovingly clean it and oil the gears and pedals, the ritual preserving what felt like freedom to him. A year later, Joe received a notice to bring the bicycle to a local warehouse. He didn't know why. It turned out that the Polish army needed all bicycles for the soldiers' transportation. With tears in his eyes, Joe stood in line, waiting to hand over the bike to a civilian, who tried to comfort him as he took the bike from Joe. As he walked away, Joe glanced back over his shoulder for one last look at his bike, which had now joined many, many others, all lined up next to each other, each with a promissory note, with the names and addresses of the children and adults who would never see them again.

It was just a bike, but it somehow became for him everything that was gone. He wrapped himself now in the pain of all of these memories, dreading to remember, dreading more to forget.

Evening eventually came, and with it the much-too-early dark of January. Shaking himself out of the sleepy fog of those hours, Joe realized that he'd have to make his way back out now if he wanted to blend back in with the workers that had left that morning. It seemed years since he had seen his father, decades since he had taken the advice his father had given him in the hopes of protecting him, the last remaining shred of what a father could do for a son in this absurd world.

He just wanted to hug him now, to hold on to him.

From his hiding-place, Joe heard the hoarse voices of the returned workers, milling around in the street by the foundry in exhausted droves. He knew his father was down there, and knew that it wouldn't take long for him and the other workers to learn what had happened earlier that day. The blood was still fresh on the street. His father would be sick with worry.

He slipped back onto the stairs, and then down, one flight at a time. Now six o'clock, the headquarters were beginning to empty out. He heard voices, though, of those who stayed to work through dinner and into the night.

They peered over their desks, haggard and full of purpose. Stamped papers, placed them in folders, transferred the folders to filing cabinets. Joe watched and waited, until all backs were turned, all heads were bowed. And then he quietly let himself out the same door he had walked in eight hours earlier.

Thirty minutes later, he and his father found each other.

"Juszo! Thank God you're all right." He hugged Joe fiercely. "How did you manage to escape?"

And then he told him. He told him how he had done the only thing he thought he could do: go where no one would expect him to be.

His father smiled, a mix of relief and pride and pain.

"I never, ever would have thought to do that."

"Let's not step forward," Joe begged his father.

"They'll never know if we don't. They'll never miss us, there's too many people out here for them to know."

Joe and his father stood in formation with the other members of the Little Ghetto—several thousand men and women—in the plaza in the late morning sun.

"Everyone who lives at Nadrzeczna 86 and 88, step forward," the German officers ordered again. They stood facing the crowd, a squad of fifty or sixty officers. Behind them, on the other side of the plaza, was a line of heavy, open-backed trucks.

Word spread quickly that the Nazis had discovered a tunnel that ran from this building to the world outside of the Ghetto. The Jewish Underground had been using it to smuggle goods in and people out. Joe had had no idea it was there, even though it had been right under his feet. It didn't matter now to the Germans whether they knew or didn't know, whether they took part in the smuggling or didn't take part: anyone living in the building was assumed to be part of a plot to sabotage them.

Joe wished he had been.

Several people stepped forward, Joe's neighbors, into the middle of the U-shaped formation. They quietly pushed their way through three, four, five rows of men.

"Let's just stay here," Joe said again.

His father was considering the idea when a kapo came up to them.

"You live there," he hissed, "you'd better come forward."

Bastard, Joe thought, shooting him a dirty look.

"Wise guy, huh?" the kapo said, smugly wrapping himself in the (false) comfort that he would be spared if he collaborated with the Nazis. (He wouldn't be).

"We'd better go forward," Joe's father whispered to Joe. "If we don't, he'll point us out to the guards and it will be worse for us."

He gestured with his thumb to the kapo, who was now moving away from them, in the direction of the guards.

They made their way to the middle of the formation and stood there for a few minutes with the others, watching the group assemble. Then guards surrounded them, forcing the group to the other side of the plaza, where the trucks were waiting.

"Onto the trucks!" the guards barked suddenly. They never spoke softly.

Joe and his father were loaded onto an already full truck, crowded against forty or fifty other men. The guards lifted the tailgate and locked it against the pressure of their packed-in bodies. They stood there, elbow-to-elbow, no room to sit down, no room even to move.

Then the truck pulled away. German police rode behind it in an open car, pointing their rifles at the line of trucks ahead of them.

Joe turned to his father. "Where are we going?"

His father shook his head—slowly at first, then vigorously, as if shaking away the only possibility.

The truck turned onto a paved, two-lane highway. It was an unfamiliar road to Joe, but the rising panic inside the truck and the shouts of the Poles who stood jeering along the road quickly made it clear to him where they were headed.

"*Jedzecie na cmentasz!*—You're going to the cemetery!"

"*Zydzi zostana zabici!*—The Jews are going to die!"

"*Zuc wasze pieniodze!*—Throw us your money! You won't need it, the Germans are going to kill you!"

Joe watched as men around him tore up their money, throwing it out of the trucks so that it would be of no use to anyone.

The panic grew wilder. People pushed, cried, screamed. Prayers and shouts crisscrossed, tangled up in one another.

"*Shema Yisrael, Adonai Eloheinu.*"

"We're going to die!"

"My wife! My children!"

"*Adonai Echad.*"

The truck drove on, nearing the cemetery. People pushed more persistently, more defiantly. Joe and his father were jostled and pressed against the tailgate of the truck. It suddenly fell open. No time for discussion, they took the only chance they both sensed they had.

Joe's father jumped. Joe followed instantly. Other men jumped, some fell out behind them.

Not missing a beat, the police open fired, spraying bullets everywhere. They shot at everyone—at the people running frantically on the ground and at those who remained huddled on the truck.

The noise was deafening: Germans shouting, Jews screaming, shots tearing through flesh and sky. Bodies fell to the ground in crashing waves.

Joe flattened himself against the pavement, lay completely still in the middle of the road. Pretended he had been hit, pretended he was dead. He kept his eyes closed as loosely as he could, afraid that a flutter of his eyelid would attract a bullet.

He lay there breathing shallow, hidden breaths. He heard the trucks stop, heard more shouts and more shots fired. Endless moments later, he heard the convoy drive away.

Slowly, tentatively, he opened one eye. Everyone was gone. No trucks, no guards. Not a living soul. He got to his feet, the only one standing in a sea of scattered bodies.

**

Joe was entirely alone now. He had just left his father's corpse, kissing him on the forehead. There was no time to say *Kaddish*, no time to mourn. Mourning would have to come later—or never come at all.

Now he had to disappear. The trucks would be back soon. He stood for a moment in the blood-spattered road, surveying his surroundings and weighing his options, which were limited. A few yards away was an apartment building, one-story, with doors opening up to a central corridor. It looked deserted. Joe dashed to the entrance, then to a ladder and climbed up to the top. Here, above the apartments, he found an attic. Making his way quietly to the darkest corner, he sat down and tried to catch his breath. Knees bent, head crumpled between them, arms crossed over as if shielding himself from the bullets that had just killed his father, Joe wept silently. He was fully aware that anything other than silence would put him in danger; he was just as aware that, were he to allow himself to release the wails that were lodged in his throat, they might never stop. Then he would be lost. Not for the first time, but now, in the first hour of his imposed solitude, he recognized how closely silence and restraint were linked to preservation.

A few minutes later, Joe heard people emerging from the seemingly-deserted apartments. They gathered in the corridor, abuzz with excitement and fear.

"Did you see those trucks?" one man asked.

"Yes, all of those Jews—off to the cemetery!" another answered

"Not all of them! Did you see how they toppled off of the truck?"

"And then *bang-bang*! The Germans took care of that!"

"I think I saw one escape."

"*Tak*," said another, "I saw a *Zyd*—a Jew—moving around, and now he's not there."

"Where did he go?"

"I think he came into our building!"

Joe heard panic in that voice.

"Where?"

"Maybe someone should go and look in the attic."

Joe held his breath, heart pounding in his throat.

"Why don't you go up and check?" asked another.

Joe closed his eyes, concentrating, making sure not to miss a word, ready to move.

"Not me! I'm not going up there!"

"What are you, afraid of a *Zyd*?"

"Me? Afraid of a *Zyd*? Forget it! But if the Germans come back and find us holding one, they'll think we're hiding him—and then we'll all be dead."

Joe opened his eyes and let his breath out. The Poles' reasoning was to his advantage. This was something he could work with.

I have to act now, he thought to himself. He ran down the ladder and headed for the door.

"*Matka boska*!" the Poles shouted, turning white and crossing themselves. "Jesus Christ!"

"He was up there the whole time!"

One of them grabbed Joe by the shoulder. "Who are you? Where have you come from?"

"I'm a Jew," he answered boldly. "I jumped from the truck."

"We'll turn him over to the Germans!" cried another.

"Then you'll die with me," Joe spat out, reminding them of what they had said earlier. "You and your wives and your children will all die. Let me go and don't say anything, and no one will get hurt. Keep me here, and we'll all be killed."

The Poles were silent, considering the logic of the argument. The one holding Joe's arm loosened his grip.

Joe ran.

Out of the building, toward a sprawling cornfield, as fast as he possibly could. He sprinted past the bodies of his father and the others, tempted to slow down, to see his father one last time. But he squelched the urge, instead deliberately locking his gaze straight ahead, denying his peripheral vision a lingering glimpse of his father. His legs carried him into the field, where he quickly dropped to his hands and knees and began to crawl. It was July, so the stalks, thankfully, were tall, easily seven feet, and he was able to stay low under them. Tassels smacked him, then disintegrated, producing clouds of dusty gnats that swirled around him. He moved deep into the cornfield, where he found a tiny clearing and sat down on the ground, relaxing slightly.

I'll hide here until it gets dark, he decided.

The short respite was interrupted when two Poles grabbed his arms. Young kids, teenagers, they had spotted Joe running into the cornfield and come looking for him. Now they had caught him off guard.

"*Zyd*," said one, "we're going to turn you in for a kilo of sugar."

Joe tried the strategy that had worked earlier: "You're not turning me in. The Nazis will think we're together. If I die, we all die."

Completely un-fazed by this, they held on to him more tightly, pushing and pulling him back towards the mouth of the field where he had entered. He struggled, planted his feet squarely on the ground, squatting slightly to add more weight. Then all at once he jerked to the left. They lost their grip and he managed to twist himself free. Arms pumping, fists clenched, thighs searing, Joe ran again. Primal fear, honed by years of running track in school, propelled him so far ahead of them that they lost his trail. When was sure he was out of sight, he collapsed in a row of corn.

He sank into the earth, controlling his breath so that he wouldn't pant too loudly.

Silence, again. Blessed, dreaded, silence.

But, just like that, it was broken. Polish and German voices placed Joe back on red-alert.

"The *Jude* was here." Joe recognized this voice; it belonged to one of the young Poles who had caught him earlier. Joe guessed that "Jude" was probably the only word he knew in German, and certainly the most useful one. It might get him a kilo of sugar.

"Where is he?" barked a deeper voice in German—probably a policeman.

They were so close to him now, he could hear their breathing. Joe put his hand over his mouth, forcing his own breath back in. One more step to the right and they would be touching him. Crouching rigidly in the corn, his whole body tensed and ready to sprint, he tasted the dirt that had accumulated in his throat during the earlier chase. He willed himself invisible, undetectable.

"He was here! The lousy *Jude* was right here!" the Poles insisted.

Defeated, annoyed, they moved past him through the towering corn.

He slowly let his breath out, wondering how it was possible that they hadn't sensed him there, huddling in the row of corn next to them.

Thank God. Oh my God. Thank you. The words played over and over in his head, a refrain of gratitude and relief and disbelief.

**

Joe lay motionless in the cornfield the entire day. Afraid to sleep, to move a muscle, to do anything that would betray him, he just lay there thinking about his next step. He pictured the Poles finding him there, dragging him out, turning him over to the Germans, who would shoot him on the spot. The Poles would receive a kilo of sugar in return. Or, they wouldn't. Either way, he'd be dead. He knew for certain that there was nobody in the surrounding houses that he could trust.

His thoughts found their way to the Rakow steel factory, a work camp several miles outside of Czestochowa. During his time in the little ghetto, people talked often about where other Jewish prisoners were being sent, and about what happened to them once they got there. He knew that the Jews that were sent to Rakow were slave laborers, but they weren't being killed… yet. Slave labor sounded better at this point than trying to survive alone, out in the open, day after day. But first, he had to figure out exactly where he was, and how to get from there to Rakow. He knew he couldn't be far, and had a general notion of which direction to take. Nearing evening, it was dark enough for Joe to feel safe walking upright through the neat rows of towering corn stalks. A long walk later, he was close to the factory grounds. He waited at the edge of the cornfields for the full cover of darkness.

When the sun was finally gone from the sky, Joe crept out of the fields and approached the work camp. There were cement walls all around, topped off by barbed-wire fencing to keep the prisoners inside. The main gate was heavily guarded. Impossible to just walk in there. He'd have to figure out another way.

Joe walked back into the cornfield and made his way around the perimeter of the camp, scanning for an unguarded entrance. There were none. His heart beat faster as he spotted a possible way in: a creek that flowed under the factory wall. This was it, his only chance.

Holding his breath, he ducked into the water and began to make his way under the wall. The steel poles that bolstered the wall and were anchored to the bottom of the creek briefly detained him. But Joe was young and skinny, and smaller than the adult prisoners for whom the camp was intended. He squeezed through the bars and came up on the other side of the wall, within the factory compound. As his head surfaced, he looked around carefully. Seeing no one, he pulled himself out of the water and began walking, dripping wet, toward the barracks.

He froze when a gruff voice accosted him in accented German.

"What are you doing here?"

It was a Ukrainian guard.

"Who are you? Where did you come from? What are you doing here?"

Joe pretended not to understand his words. But he couldn't ignore his rifle.

"You're not from this camp," the guard informed him. "Everyone from this camp is accounted for. They count heads here every day and every night to make sure no one's missing. Tell me the truth or I'll take you to police headquarters, and you know what that means."

Yes, he knew what that meant. But what else could he do? He continued to pretend he didn't understand.

"Come with me," the guard ordered, exasperated.

He followed the guard to police headquarters.

"We've got a Jew," the guard told another. "Get the commandant."

Joe stood there, poker-faced. Inside, he was reeling. This hadn't been the plan. The plan had been to sneak in here and blend in with the workers unnoticed. Now he had no idea what to do.

A man came in then—not the German officer in charge of the camp, but the Jew in charge of the Jewish workers. Some of the Jewish workers had watched Joe being marched to police headquarters, and they had gone to tell this *kapo*.

He recognized Joe from Czestochowa.

"I'm Kantor," he told Joe quickly in Polish. "I knew your father. You escaped from the ghetto?"

"Yes," Joe told him, "I escaped from a truck. They were taking us to the cemetery. My father is dead."

Kantor shook his head sadly. "I'm sorry. He was a good man. But how did you get in here?"

"I came under the wall, where the stream is," Joe answered. "And then I got caught coming up on the inside of the camp."

"Okay, " Kantor said. "Here's what you'll do: whatever the commandant asks you, tell him the truth. He'll be able to tell if you're lying, and he doesn't let liars live. I'll see what I can do to keep you here, alive."

Joe wasn't a particularly good liar anyway, but he wondered how the truth could save him.

The commandant came in. Kantor spoke with him in German.

"Mr. Miloff," he said, "this young man smuggled himself into the factory so that he can work for you." He repeated Joe's story, emphasizing that he wanted to work for the Germans.

Miloff turned to Joe then, asking him in German, "What's your name?"

"Joseph Koenigheit, sir."

"Koenigheit? That's a German name."

"Yes, sir, it is. But I'm Jewish."

Kantor translated from Polish to German as Joe spoke.

"Did your father ever live in Germany?" Miloff asked.

"Yes, sir. He went to college there and he worked there." Joe didn't know much more than that about his father's time in Germany. It was before he was married, and he didn't talk about it much.

"And you," he asked, "you escaped from the ghetto? From the selection?" He knew that there had been one.

Joe told him the truth. About how he had jumped from the truck. About his father. About his narrow escape. The truth was heart-wrenching enough, but Joe related it as pathetically as he could.

"And you snuck into Rakow?" Something like admiration was unmistakable in Miloff's face.

"Yes, sir."

"Why?"

Then Joe did lie:

"Because I want to work for you, sir," he told him. "I want to contribute to your efforts. Your country. Your government."

Miloff knew he was being charmed, but at this point didn't seem to mind. This kid impressed him, and he didn't much have the stomach for the sort of work his fellow Nazis were doing in the ghetto. Caught in the machinery of war, he didn't share the fatal will-to-power that fueled it. He embraced an opportunity to look the other way.

"How old are you, boy?" he asked Joe.

"Fifteen, sir." Joe could sense him softening.

"You look like a nice kid. We like people like you," he said to Joe.

He turned to Kantor: "What do you think?"

Kantor took responsibility for Joe, assuring Miloff that he was from a good family, and that, if he said he wanted to work, he would work.

"Okay, then. Go with Kantor," Miloff said. "*Fahr schwinden*—get out of my sight. Don't let me see you here again," he added, counting "*Ein, zwei, drei*!" just to sharpen his point.

"Thank you, sir. Thank you," Joe said, fleeing from the room as quickly as he could.

Kantor came out a moment later. "Good for you, " he told Joe. "You're a lucky guy. They seldom let a guy in your situation live. See, he liked you because you told the truth."

"You saved my life, sir. Thank you," Joe told him, unsure if his words conveyed his gratitude, hoping that they did.

Kantor took Joe to the barracks. He talked to another Jewish worker who was a camp manager.

"Kopinski," Kantor said to the man, "I'm assigning this kid to your barracks. You're in charge of him now."

Joe looked around. He saw familiar faces from the Czestochowa Ghetto. Many of these men had seen him get on the truck that morning. They were surprised to see him.

"Where did that truck go?" they asked him.

"To the cemetery," Joe told them.

They understood.

"I'm Klobucki now," Joe said to himself as soon as he had his bearings in the Rakow barracks. Miloff hadn't written his name down; there were no records of a Joseph Koenigheit at the camp, and Joe wanted to keep it that way. He was well aware of the German strategy of making people disappear: they came at night, pulled you out of your bed and never brought you back. If word got out that he had escaped that truck ride to the cemetery, if somehow he were associated with the ghetto underground (the false association that had landed him on the truck in the first place), things would get very bad for him indeed.

At this point, the name change was largely symbolic, a security measure so that, when he would need to assume a new identity—in places where it would mean certain death to be a Jew—he would have it ready at his fingertips. Insurance against the fatal condition of being caught off-guard or flustered. In the relative protection of this place and in the privacy of his own head, he tried on this typical Polish name, testing its fit against his Jewish skin. He was surprised how little it chafed against him, necessity apparently diminishing his attachment to his own name.

Here, there were still people who knew exactly who Joe was. People like the camp doctor, Glater, who knew his family. Who knew the prominent place his father, Theodore, used to hold in the Czestochowa community; the manager of some of the largest residential buildings and rental properties in the city, virtually everyone knew him. Everyone who did liked and respected him for his professionalism and integrity. On Saturdays, Joe would go with him to visit the properties he managed, basking in the glow of being the well-liked manager's son. Later, after the war started, he felt a more tempered pride when he accompanied his father to Gidle, the work camp outside of Czestochowa, where his father—fluent in German—had been assigned the position of camp manager. There, he had enjoyed the special privileges (everything is relative) and the small consolation of being the manager's son. It was from Gidle that Joe returned with his father to the ghetto, to find that his mother and sisters were gone—taken with so many others to Treblinka. They had heard rumors about Treblinka in Gidle. There was no reason to hope they were alive.

Here, there were still people who knew his mother, Sarah. Who knew what a gracious woman and exceptional mother she was, how she would get up every morning at the crack of dawn to arrive at the bakery before it opened at 5 a.m., so that she could buy bread, round rolls, or bagels, before anyone else touched them. It was a long walk there and back to their apartment, but she would do it every morning so that there would be fresh bread on the table for Joe and his sisters by the time they got up for school. People who knew that her whole life was her kids, was building a home around and for them that made them feel safe and loved and secure in the knowledge that this was their home.

There weren't many people at Rakow who knew these things, but that there were any gave Joe the smallest shred of comfort, dulling ever-so-slightly the bruising ache of his grief. And, as it turned out, he had family here. Cousins—Juzek and Janek—who arrived a few months earlier. In his bunk, fully clothed, Joe lay down and covered himself with a coarse blanket. As he had before, he reflected now on how lucky he had been, under the circumstances. *I have cousins, I have shelter, and I have a place to lie down and straighten out,* he thought, counting his blessings and pulling the blanket more tightly around him.

The Nazis came for his cousins one night, pulling them out of their bunk—too far from Joe's own to hear them. Someone had fingered them as members of the underground. They were shot in the darkness.

The ache returned.

Though he was not mechanically inclined, Joe was taken to the mechanical department at Rakow. This was lucky, given the other options: like shoveling coal off of endless freight cars all day in all kinds of weather, or feeding coal to the immense ovens that powered the factory day and night, or cleaning the barracks and wretched-smelling outhouse that served all of the prisoners. Here, he was one of very few Jews—four or five among at least a hundred Poles who were paid for their work, and who came in the morning and left in the evening. They brought metal lunchboxes from home every day; many snuck food to Joe despite the enormous risk to them and him. Had they been caught, they would have been fired and Joe, shot. For him, the risk was worth it—he was starving and could trade whatever food he didn't eat for decent shoes and clothes that fit. And, having done it before, he was relatively confident in his ability to talk himself out of trouble, if it found him. As for them, he couldn't fathom why they would put themselves in danger—for him. He chalked it up to the fact that he was younger than everyone else, and clearly on his own.

He took it as it came, having learned that to care too deeply about others' reasons and motivations was a waste of energy.

His lack of mechanical skill generally acknowledged, Joe managed to land a position as a kind of freelancer, a general-purpose assistant, assigned to whatever job came up. He swept the floor, helped move finished jobs from one place to another, and brought parts to the machine workers. Unlike the other positions that chained a prisoner to a specific task and spot, Joe had some freedom of movement. And he had some measure of responsibility: he was in charge of the supply closet during the day; he would take the key from a hook in the director's office in the morning and hang it back up when he left at night.

The director in charge of the mechanical department was a German engineer named Eden. He was a well-known sonofabitch, a short and stubby man who terrorized his workers. "Back to work!" he'd scream if he saw them standing still for even a moment, eyes bulging and veins popping out of his neck. Usually he wore a white lab coat, but occasionally—to remind his workers who they were dealing with—he would wear his Nazi uniform, the swastika armband announcing his entirely unearned but lethal power.

Eden was a bastard, but he was also rather predictable. At least, his schedule was, and Joe had him figured out pretty quickly. As long as he appeared to be working when Eden was around, there was no problem. So Joe did this, masterfully engaged in his own performance. Pretty soon, Joe was watching Eden more than Eden was watching him, turning the tables on this man who remained oblivious to his shrinking sphere of control. Joe carried a broom with him at all times, sweeping furiously when he saw Eden, and resting as soon as his eyes were turned. He soon discovered that he could disappear behind a machine or into a corner, or, even better, that he could hide away for longer. Always exhausted from the grueling ritual and meager provisions of the camp, Joe learned when Eden would be away at lunch or a meeting, and then he would nap in the broom closet, which he locked from the inside. Or, he slipped into the restroom, where he napped—sitting on a toilet—before washing up as best as he could in the sink, drying himself with the old newspaper placed there for this purpose.

Joe played it perfectly, timing his emergence from the closet or restroom carefully to coincide with Eden's return. Eden never caught on.

Joe settled in.

**

Rakow closed on a cold January morning in 1945. On orders of the Ukrainian guards who policed the camp, the Jewish prisoners gathered near the train track formerly used to bring coal for the metallurgy. Unsure of where they were going, certain only of their own powerlessness, they stood there, waiting.

The guards divided them into two groups, leading each to a separate set of cattle cars. Joe walked with the others onto a closed car, people crowding around him, pressing against him, squeezing into a space that had been filled to capacity ten times over. No room to sit down, no seats even if there had been. The doors shut behind them, locks clicking into position without remorse. It went dark inside the car, save for a sliver of light delivered through the barbed wire of the tiny window on the top corner of the car. The same window offered a breath of air, stingily parceled out among them. The whole car was filled with noxious sweat and the unmistakable stench of human waste. Bodies responding unwillingly and reflexively to conditions designed to produce exactly these results. This, Joe realized, was what people must have meant when they said they could smell fear.

In the midst of all of these bodies, many passing imperceptibly from dehumanization to death at some point during the two-day journey, Joe stood alone. As he had been from the moment of his father's death, now more than a year and a half ago. Around him, people wept, moaned, starved, suffocated.

He trained his thoughts elsewhere, on the practicalities of the situation. He thought through what it meant that he was here on this train:

If they're taking us out of Rakow it means that this all has to be ending soon. They used us for free labor there, forcing us to work toward the war effort. If they're shutting down Rakow, they're probably shutting down other slave labor camps, too. And that means they don't need us to work for them anymore. If the Germans were winning the war, they'd still need us. The end has to be close.

Alone with these thoughts, he felt strangely hopeful. All he had to do was stay alive. To make it to the end that was surely coming soon.

He could do that.

**

"*Raus! Raus!*—Get out! Get out!

Joe was jolted out of a fitful standing sleep by the command and the clunk of the cattle car door sliding open. He stumbled with the others off the train, weaving a path through bodies, rubbing his eyes at the sudden light. The air was cold, crisp with an electric clarity.

He didn't know exactly where he was, but the unmediated, unforgiving scent of death that greeted them gave him a pretty good idea. He had heard about concentration camps, the stuff of rumors and panicked whispers in the little ghetto and Rakow. Now, as the German soldiers counted and separated the prisoners into groups and marched them into the camp enclosed in a barbed-wire fence, there could be no doubt.

Joe marched with the others through the main gate that read *Jedem das Seine*—"to each his own"—twisted ruthlessly in the Nazi universe to mean "everyone gets what he deserves." This place, he learned quickly, was Buchenwald. Transports arrived here from all over Europe, trainloads upon trainloads every day. Some went straight to the crematoria. As the Allied Forces got closer in the months that followed, the Germans turned to execution, herding prisoners by the hundreds, then thousands, into the forest beyond the camp, into mass graves in they had been forced to dig, shooting them and burning their bodies.

The guards marched Joe's group to Bloc 65, a barracks indistinguishable from the rest, with bunks made of wood, attached by posts in the corners. No sheets, no mattresses, no room at all to lie down. Joe was assigned to an upper bunk with four other men, a space that was built for one.

"This is your home," the guard told them coldly. "You're going to live here and work here."

Not for long, Joe thought to himself with a promise and a shrug.

At 6:00 am every morning, a polka-blaring PA woke the prisoners. Each bloc released its 200-250 prisoners to the courtyard outside the barracks, where they reassembled in rows ten deep by ten across for roll call. All heads were counted, all accounted for. If a head was missing, there was hell to pay. His first morning, Joe was assigned to "broom detail"—charged with the daily, endless, and superfluous task of keeping the surroundings of the barracks clean.

The brutal conditions at Buchenwald took Joe by surprise. Rakow had been no picnic, but this was something else entirely. Unrelenting hunger, so deep it penetrated bone, produced a host of unwelcome results. Beyond the physical—from dysentery to violent starvation—hunger demanded choices and behavior a full stomach might cast aside as unthinkable. Impossible to rest easy here, impossible to dismiss what could keep you alive.

The chain of command here was inflexible and understood, and constructed to create the appearance of its own legitimacy. Each bloc was assigned to a German officer who had ultimate power over the prisoners; the day-to-day affairs were handled by the *blocowy*—generally a Polish national—who answered to the German officer. Joe's *blocowy* was a Polish national, a political prisoner who had gotten on the wrong side of the Nazis. He was an intelligent and educated man, of average height, around forty years old. The Germans had granted him his own room and four assistants—political prisoners: two Belgians, one Hungarian, and one Frenchman—to help him manage the barracks. Like the *blocowy*, they enjoyed far better accommodations than the Jewish prisoners; their political differences with the Germans had not stood in the way of their sharing a small room together, each with their own bunk. They were also permitted to receive care packages from their families and the Red Cross. This reliable supply of food and cigarettes meant they were never hungry or far from the meager release that nicotine promised.

Joe learned quickly that connections were everything here. A *kibbitzer* by nature, a people person, Joe leaned heavily into it now, in single-minded pursuit of friendship with the *blocowy* and his assistants. It wasn't hard to come by; the *blocowy* enjoyed talking with Joe and took an instant liking to him. And he felt protective of him, this cheerful-seeming seventeen year old who spoke such beautiful Polish (much better than his own) and who was so completely alone. Soon, his four assistants felt the same way. They took Joe under their wing, inviting him to sit with them in their room in the evening, sharing their food with him, speaking with him in German to include him in the conversation (Joe didn't speak French, the language they normally used with one another), extending the tangible and intangible shelter of special dispensation over his head.

In return—though no return was demanded of him—Joe took on the role of valet. He cleaned their room, took out their garbage, swept the floor.

"You don't have to do that," they'd tell him as he hauled a bag of trash out the door.

"That's okay," Joe would answer. "No big deal."

And it wasn't. It was the least he could do, he figured.

They stuck to small talk:

"What did you do before the war?"

"Where are you from?"

"How did you live?"

"What kind of family did you have?"

Nothing political. Ever. It was the unspoken rule. Caution reigned; no cards revealed. Impossible to know who's who under these conditions.

And no jokes. There was nothing to joke about.

A crowd of inmates stood waiting for Joe outside the door of the room.

"Do you have anything for us?" they'd ask, eagerly, expectantly.

He'd give them what he could—a piece of salami, some bread, some cake. Whatever he had been able to stash away. Or, temporarily sated from his friends' offerings, he would offer over his own watery soup to someone else. Someone who was hungrier.

"All Jewish prisoners must report tomorrow to the plaza for a count."

Joe was in the barracks when the announcement came. His hackles went up. This was not a good sign.

He went to his friend, the *blocowy*.

"What should I do?" Joe asked him. "Do you think I should go out there or not?"

"No," the *blocowy* told him. "Tomorrow, when the Jews report, you'll stay in my room. If they call the rest of the prisoners, I'll have to go out, too. If this happens, you'll follow me. Stay close to me. Keep your eyes on me. Do what I do. I won't keep an eye on you, okay? You keep an eye on me, and I'll let you know what you should do."

The next day the Jewish prisoners went out. They didn't come back. Bloc 65 was empty.

Joe followed his *blocowy* like a shadow.

Two days later there was another announcement: all non-Jews—Russians, gypsies, political prisoners, everyone—must report immediately to the public square. The camp was being emptied of all its prisoners.

"You come out with me, " Joe's *blocowy* told him. "Now you're no longer a Jew; you're a Pole like me."

Joe stepped into the name he had chosen at Rakow—Klobucki—and into the Polish division on the square.

They marched out of the camp in one long column, ten prisoners across and several hundred deep, German officers flanking them. In the freezing cold, nothing to wrap around them for warmth, heavy shoes with soles made of wood or no soles at all, they marched through the day and into the night and back again.

People fell to the ground in exhaustion, unable to go any farther. They were shot on the spot. Bodies piled up on each side of the road as the column moved on at a steady pace. Impossible to stop and help; a gesture of empathy answered by a bullet to the head.

When the German officers needed a rest, they stopped the march for a few hours. Joe lay on the cold ground with the other prisoners, curling his body around him as tightly as he could. A fitful but grateful respite.

Then, suddenly, "Everybody up on your feet!"

And then the death march resumed.

To the right of the paved highway they marched on was a forest dense with trees. Joe kept his eyes glued on the *blocowy*, staying near him. Without any warning, escaping the notice of the German officers, the *blocowy* darted with several other men into the forest. Joe looked around quickly and did the same thing. Heart racing madly, he ran into the forest as fast as he could, half expecting the shot that would stop him in his tracks.

He made it into the forest. He breathed an abbreviated sigh of relief, realizing that the *blocowy* and the others had disappeared. Too risky to shout out for them, Joe sat silently in the dark, wondering, worrying, weighing his options. Alone with his set of choiceless choices. He could stay here, at the mercy of the unknown, or he could rejoin the column of prisoners. As he had once before, when he opted to sneak into Rakow, he calculated now that he would be better off in the company of others than fending for himself in the dark.

No one noticed him when he quickly and quietly stepped back into formation. Seventeen years old, he chose the hell he knew.

Two weeks later, a brutally diminished group arrived at Flossenburg, a Nazi work camp that had—until recently—been reserved for
political prisoners and criminals. In 1942, under orders of the SS, the
handful of Jewish prisoners who were housed there were sent to Auschwitz. Flossenburg was *judenfrei*—free of Jews—until late summer of
1944, when the Nazi war machine began to implode in response to
D-Day. Now, thousands of Jews descended upon this notoriously fierce
population of criminals (most of them rabid anti-Semites).

Joe clung to his assumed identity.

The accommodations were a slight improvement over Buchenwald:
in bunks of three or four, each with a blanket, at least a person could
sleep here. Joe was assigned to a barracks filled with young Polish na-
tionals, members of the Polish underground. Nineteen and twenty-year
old guys who had taken part in the Warsaw Uprising. Tough guys. Really tough.

"Are you Jewish?" some of the more vicious ones asked Joe one day.

Shit, he thought. This was bad.

"No," he answered. "Why would you ask that?"

"Because we think you are. You look like a Jew. You smell like a Jew."

They gathered around him now, right up in his face.

Joe let loose a string of creative and complicated obscenities in Polish. This should have ended the discussion. In Yiddish, maybe, a Jew
would talk like this. But not Polish.

It just wasn't done.

They still weren't convinced.

"I don't care how well you speak Polish," one guy insisted, "I think
you're a dirty, stinking Jew." He shoved Joe.

Joe shoved him back.

"What you think and what I say are two different things."

"So what?"

"So, you bastard," Joe went on, trying to put him on the defensive.
"So you must have done something wrong if you're in here."

"Yeah, well let's just see." The group moved closer, menacing now.
"Let's go to the washroom. You pull your pants down, we'll see who's a

Jew, clear as day."

"Why don't you pull *your* pants down, you bunch of jackasses. The only ones I'll pull my pants down for are the Germans. Who the hell do you people think you are? You go to hell!"

Joe was completely bluffing now, remembering how his cousin, a boxer, would puff himself up during a fight and imitating him as best he could. He weaved and bobbed, deflecting the taunts as if they were blows.

A few other guys, tired of this bullying when so much else was at stake, came to Joe's defense.

"Leave him alone," they said. "He told you he's not a Jew, so leave him alone."

"We don't believe him," the bullies protested.

"Who cares? Whether you believe him or not, leave him alone. What's the big deal?"

One of them turned to Joe:

"Don't worry about it, kid," he said. "You're a smart guy. Don't worry about it."

Joe smiled in response, then shot a grin of vindication at the bullies.

"Yeah, well, I still don't believe you." One last, weak, accusation, a necessary show of machismo.

"Yeah, well, I'm not Jewish, whether you like it or not. And if you ever start with me again, I'll punch you so hard you won't see straight for a week."

They never mentioned it again.

**

Days later, the now-familiar announcement was broadcast over the PA: "Everybody must report to the plaza. Immediately."

Roll call, then the guards marched everyone out.

"You're not coming back here," they said.

Another death march had begun. As before, the prisoners rested on the cold ground only when the guards were tired. As before, the bodies piled up, grotesque and indiscriminate. Those who couldn't keep up—feet, hearts, wills spent—collapsed and were shot (unless it was abundantly clear that they were already dead, in which case it made no sense to waste a bullet).

One week later, those who were still alive arrived at Dachau. The end of the road.

April 29, 1945. Liberation.

**

I wouldn't go back to Częstochowa if they paid me, Joe thought, reeling with the knowledge that his family was gone. He had sent in papers to the Red Cross in Germany, listing the names and former addresses of his relatives.

Nothing.

There was no one else he could think of who might still be in Europe. No reason at all to go back to Poland, cesspool of anti-Semitism that it still remained. Seventeen years old, he wrestled with the most basic questions: *Where do I go? What do I do? How can I find my way back to a normal life?*

A few days after liberation, he was approached by a band of soldiers who wore the khaki uniform of the British army, patches on the shoulders reading "Palestine."

"Don't be afraid," they told Joe and the group of young men he was standing with. "We're the Jewish Brigade. Who wants to go to Palestine?"

"You sit in front with me," the driver told Joe. He was a Palestinian Jew, originally from Hungary.

They were leaving Dachau after two weeks of recuperation. The Jewish Brigade had taken Joe and the group of teenagers who chose to join them under their wing: feeding and clothing them, and setting up temporary housing in abandoned buildings of the camp. Joe and the others threw their striped prisoner's uniforms in the garbage, proudly and gratefully replacing them with whatever clothing the Brigade found for them.

Now, Joe sat in the cab of a big British Army truck, alone with the driver and another soldier, while the other kids lay hidden under tarpaulins in the back. He wasn't sure why he had been singled out—perhaps because he was wearing everything that the soldiers were wearing: green army pants, an army shirt, a khaki sweater—but he was excited nevertheless. When border patrol looked inside the cab—as they surely would—they would think Joe was a member of the Brigade.

They arrived at the German-Italian border at night, prepared to smuggle the Jewish refugees filling the backs of the line of trucks past the Italian police. As it turned out, the Italian police didn't raise a finger to stop them. Not so much as even checking the front of the truck that Joe sat in so eagerly, they let the entire convoy through the border. Perhaps a simple matter of bribery, perhaps an attempt to make amends for caving into Hitler's murderous regime, the Italian government—border patrol its most visible face—did little in these early days after the war to present an obstacle to the Jews they had a hand in displacing.

The convoy now made its way to Santa Maria, where the Brigade had a facility for the kids they were taking to Israel. There they would stay until the proper certification came from the British government to allow them entrance into Palestine.

For seven months—until November, 1945, when the papers came authorizing the legal emigration of this first wave of children survivors to Palestine—Joe stayed in Italy. Hebrew classes and discussions about Israeli history and culture in the morning, afternoons and evenings entirely free to do what he wanted. Swimming in the sea, napping in the sun, sleeping in a bed reserved for him alone. Coming back to life. In the company of so many others who each had his or her story to tell, they chose not to tell these stories. They didn't have to.

July 17, 1927: Joe is born, to Sarah and Theodore Koenigheit, in Czestochowa.

September 1, 1939: Nazis invade Poland. Joe recalls hearing planes overhead early in the morning.

September 3, 1939: German forces occupy Czestochowa.

September 4, 1939: "Bloody Monday" Action. 300 Jews are killed in the streets of Czestochowa by Nazis.

April 9, 1941: Jewish Ghetto ("Big" Ghetto) is established in Czestochowa. Joe and his father are shipped to Gidle, a work camp, where they work in a stone quarry until 1942, when they return to Czestochowa. Joe's mother and sisters, Eva and Marisha, are left behind in the ghetto.

September 22-October 4, 1942: Large-scale deportation of Jews to Treblinka (around 39,000 people were deported, another 2,000 were shot in the streets). Joe's mother and sisters are among those deported. On the day of their deportation, Joe and his father are assigned to clean-up detail of the "Big" Ghetto.

November 1942: "Small" Ghetto is established in northeastern part of former "Big" Ghetto. Joe and his father live in this consolidated ghetto.

December 1942: Jewish Fighting Organization (ZOB) established. Their headquarters are set up in the makeshift apartment complex Joe shares with his father and several other families.

January 4, 1943: ZOB uprising against the Nazis.

January 5, 1943: Nazis shoot 127 members of the Jewish intelligentsia and 250 children and elderly people in retaliation for the uprising. This is most likely the day that Joe hides in Gestapo headquarters.

March 20, 1943: Extermination of Jewish intelligentsia (taken on trucks to the Czestochowa cemetery, they are tricked by the premise that they will be relocated to Palestine). There are several mass exterminations of this sort over the next months, all following the route to the cemetery that Joe and his father will take.

June 1943: HASAG Rakow forced labor steel mill opens. Joe will sneak into the camp shortly after its opening.

June 25, 1943: Another ZOB uprising, resisting liquidation of the "Small" Ghetto. This is most likely the impetus for the truck ride to the Czestochowa cemetery, during which Theodore Koenigheit is killed. Joe and Theodore were suspected of collaboration with the ZOB, a charge Joe denies.

June 26-30, 1943: Liquidation of the "Small" Ghetto. It is most likely June 26th that Joe flees to the cornfields of rural Czestochowa, and the late night/early morning of June 27th when he decides to sneak into Rakow.

January 16, 1945: HASAG Rakow closes; forced laborers (Joe among them) are transported to Buchenwald and Ravensbruck. Joe is taken to Buchenwald where he manages to "pass" as a Pole.

April 6-10, 1945: Evacuation of Buchenwald.

April 8, 1945: Death march to Flossenburg begins.

April 20, 1945: Death march to Dachau begins.

April 29, 1945: Liberation of Dachau. Shortly after, Joe goes to Italy with the Jewish Brigade.

PART THREE: PULLING THREADS

THINGS UNRAVEL

So now it's 2016. Elie Wiesel died last week, and this Suit, which seems so neatly sewn up, still… isn't. It has a life of its own. I'm sitting on the tattered couch in our rental house in Brunswick, Maine, where we've taken our sabbatical. There are gaping tears exposing the foam stuffing underneath, threads pulled free of the patterned fabric, the grisly aftermath of the age-old battle of dog vs. couch. Dog clearly won. We're staying down the street from my stepdad and mom, who is in the early stages of Alzheimer's and can't seem to form new memories. Our conversations spin in endless loops, an eternal return propelled, it would seem, by nagging obsession with both the minute and monumental. It seems somehow fitting to be caught now in that loop.

In the aftermath of storytelling.

On the couch next to me sits a glossy-covered, off-sized paperback, different from the one Joe's son had shown me, now so many years ago, at the brunch table in his sister's Chicago townhouse. This one bears my name and contains The Suit.

The Suit: a palimpsest, layers of voices stacked together and flattening out into one, relatively neat, story. Or maybe it's better to call it a character sketch, lovingly crafted from the fragmented drafts of others, from the energy of literature, titans of the genre—Elie Wiesel, Primo Levi, Viktor Frankl—I tried to emulate, from long and winding conversations with Joe in that glassed-in boardroom. From over-the-phone conversations from Joe's sons, responses to my own early drafts. Those pages are the product of Joe's and Joe's family's coinciding wish to preserve and collect Joe's story. For Joe, it's a matter of self-preservation: "There comes a time when you *have* to tell your story," he told me once. "Because if you keep it to yourself it will kill you." It's also a grim acknowledgment of the all-too-present reality that, soon, there will be no one left to tell the story. Joe is one of an estimated 100,000 survivors that remain alive. The youngest are around 71 years old.[7]

In a statement following Wiesel's death, the president of the Conference on Jewish Material Claims Against Germany, Julius Berman, stresses the obligation that comes in the midst of this reality: "We are losing survivors with first-hand accounts of the Holocaust every day. For this reason, it is incumbent on us to record, document and represent survivors' experiences and keep them in the public consciousness, lest we forget the depths to which society is capable of sinking."[8]

Everyone involved in the process of developing The Suit—Joe, his family, the women who prepared the fragmented early drafts, me—shares this sense of obligation to record and document. Everyone agrees, there is precious little time to waste in recording these stories. It's the issue of *representation* that I struggle so much with, and that leaves me feeling ultimately dissatisfied with The Suit as the definitive account of Joe's story. So much still feels unsaid. So many questions still hover over the process for me: *How* to tell another person's story? *How* to capture the details of what happened to Joe in a way that makes for a "good" story? And what is *the* story, after all? How to nail it down?

This, then, all that follows, is The Suit unraveling. The threads being pulled. The explicit showing of my choices and our conversations and the unexpected turns they took in my attempts to nail the story down. Because this unraveling, it seems to me, is also part of the story that needs to be told.

A quick and dirty schema, to take with us (approximations… memory is a slippery thing):

Fall 2008 (reprise): My colleague asks me if I'm interested in Joe's story, I say "yes," call his son, set up a meeting with Joe and the family. Before the meeting, Joe's son sends me two drafts of Joe's story, transcribed by other women. I read these in preparation for the meeting.

February-May 2009 (reprise +): In preparation for our first meeting, I email Joe a list of questions. A series of meetings with Joe in his son's boardroom on Wacker Drive ensues. I record most of these, and transcribe the rest (the recorder glitched a few times). A few phone calls in between: quick hellos and clarification of points raised in the drafts and in prior conversations.

May-July 2009: I draft a version of the manuscript. I talk with Joe on the phone a few times for clarification as I'm writing. And also just to hear his voice.

Late July 2009: I send the draft to Joe and his family, with a note of explanation to Joe of the approach I took.[9]

August 2009: Phone conversation with Joe's sons about the draft; they ask for additional material to be included and for me to cut details that they find superfluous.

September 2009: I compile a new draft, making the changes Joe's sons requested.

October 2009: I meet with Joe, his wife and one of his sons at a Corner Bakery near Skokie, to discuss the revised draft and additional revisions the family would like to see.

Early December 2009: I send Joe and each of his children a bound copy of the revised manuscript.

Early December 2009-now: Things fall apart with Joe's family, the acrimony of storytelling, and, in the midst of it, I lose my connection to Joe.

Early December 2009-now: I work and rework the story behind that manuscript, listening to my recordings over and over and over, listening for the story that wants to take shape, missing Joe's voice, missing our connection, haunted by all that's been left un-wrestled-with.

Hi Joe,

Hope this finds you very well!

So, this is going to be painful...
In preparation for our meeting in a few weeks, I'm going to ask you if you can recall, in as much detail as you possibly can, several moments that come up in the drafts of your story that I've read. I'm sorry to ask you to go through all of this again.

1) What was it like when you first moved into the Big Ghetto? How did you move your things from your house? How did you decide what to take? How did your parents act? What did you feel like when you first got to the ghetto with them?

2) What happened the day that you and your father were taken away to Gidle? Did you go through a selection before you went with your father? What do you remember about the trip to Gidle and when you arrived there? What about the time you spent there? What sorts of things did you and your father talk about? Who were you friendly with here? Who was in charge?

3) The day you returned to the Little Ghetto to find your mother and sisters had been taken (along with everyone else). Try to remember exactly what you were thinking, feeling. Did you know that you would never see them again?

***4) I want to know everything about that day that you stayed behind in the factory in the little ghetto. How exactly did you get out of the factory without them seeing you? Want to know every last detail about how you then got into the Gestapo headquarters. Everything. What did you see? What were people doing? Where did you go once you opened the door? How long were you hiding there? What were you thinking about while you were hiding? What did your hiding space there look like? How did you eventually get out of this building to join the workers returning? (This scene is going to be really, really important. Readers will be absolutely fascinated, so I want to make sure to set the stage as accurately as possible).

5) The scene in the courtyard just before the truck ride to the cemetery. How many people were out there? What did the man who sold you out look like? What were you thinking about this guy? Did you father say anything at any point?

6) Can you set the scene when you were hiding in the cornfield? What were you thinking? Was it sunny? Grey? Cold? Hot? How long were you sitting there holding your breath?

7) Want more about the trip to Israel. How did you get there from Italy? How long did it take? Who was with you? What did you talk about? Do? Eat?

8) Scenes of your life in the kibbutz, before you enter the army. Would like to see you interacting with other people during this time. What did you talk about? How did you spend your day? Can you show me?

***9) Scenes of you fighting in the army. This one is going to be tough... but we absolutely need to see you here. And we need to know exactly what you were doing and feeling while you were fighting. Did you go directly into battle? Did you kill anyone? This is a HUGE piece of your story... what it means for you to be a soldier after your experience in the war. You've told me that you did things that you had to do because you were a soldier, things that you might not necessarily have done otherwise. We NEED to know what these things are, and we need to re-live them along with you.

10) What do you remember about the day you came here? Everything.

11) Want to see you stationed in Trieste. What did you do there? What were your fellow soldiers like? Give me a typical day.

12) Scenes of your life here. Want to see you, for instance, at a JCC dance. Want to see you at the party where you meet your wife.

13) The return scene to Czestochowa. I want to capture, particularly, that moment when you go back to your old apartment.

This is a lot! And we probably won't get to all of it, but it will give us a place to start. One more basic question, to help us to set the scene of who you are now and who you were then:

—What do you dream about? Do you remember what you dreamed about at these various points throughout your life? What do you think these dreams mean?

Thanks so much, Joe! I'm so excited to be working with you and so looking forward to seeing you soon!

All best,
Beth

"It's *all* important," Joe corrected me as we sat, pictures spilling out of a box onto the table in front of us, me holding my numbered list of questions like a talisman to keep us on track. "You think it's not important now, but it will be."

"Oh, I know," I told him, shrugging off the embarrassment I felt for the brief glimpse he'd gotten that, despite myself, I was hearing his story selectively, perking up when he said words like "selection" or "Aktion," or "train" and losing focus when he gave complicated genealogical descriptions of how the faces in the pictures fit together.

Joe had brought that box of pictures to our first meeting in response to the onslaught of questions I'd emailed him. His intuition—dead on—that these images would ground me in the day-to-day. Now as we sat, heads together, moving from image to image, Joe pointing out the memories he'd collected, the questions receded.

Dozens of photos, hundreds. Cousins and friends in Israel, his parents, his grandparents, family members who died in the camps, Joe in a neatly pressed Israeli Army uniform (a favorite for both of us), Joe in the American Army, stationed at Trieste, an ex-girlfriend (the Hebrew inscription on her photo we deciphered together—"we will always be friends"), and one in particular that he wanted to show me, his bachelor party ("you look like you behaved yourself pretty well," I teased him. "No women jumping out of cakes or anything." "I ALWAYS behave myself!" he assured me).

Half an hour in, Joe sighs, sits back from the table, and sums up: "So you see, these are nice pictures, something to cherish. So… if you feel you that you want later to put some pictures into the book…" he trails off.

"Yes! I think we should! I think we should!"

On the recording of this conversation, there's a rustle and sharp clicking of chairs at this moment, a noticeable shift in energy. The decision to include the photos propelled us forward.

"I've got so many pictures here, so many pictures!" I hear Joe exclaim on the recording. "I've gotta do something with all of this. It's crazy. All these years, all these years… like a Polack!" He snorts, sheepishly, caught in his unmitigated prejudice. "There's so much to do here that you don't know what to do first."

"I know, Joe. I know." I hear myself tell him. "But these are so great. Thank you for showing them to me. It helps very much to see. This makes it real."

"Yes, this way you can look."

I *did* know what he meant, that feeling of not knowing where to start, of being overwhelmed. There are just so many starting points. Where does the "story" begin? What's the arc, the thread, the framing narrative? What's the way in? And the messages I got from Joe were sometimes mixed, which made it difficult to know what to focus on and how. "You want all these details, but that's not important," he'd told me when I was pushing him for scene-builders. So which was it? Was all of it important, or was none of it?

I go back to the tapes.

Sitting on the tattered couch in Brunswick, ME, wood-stove directly in front of me, windows looking onto the front porch behind me, I'm listening to the recordings of our conversations on iTunes with my finger poised over the pause icon. I force the recording back, again and again and again, returning to the same parts over and over. Listening for the arc. A Word document is open on the screen. I frantically transcribe word for word or jot down fragmented thoughts as I listen. There's something about copying the words down as I hear them that makes them stick, makes them embodied, makes me hear them in a way I'd missed before.

"So here's the thing, Joe," I hear myself saying, about an hour after he first showed me his photos. "What I have is the rough story, what I need from you is what it *felt* like. You're amazing; you don't know how amazing you are. And I'm charged with this task of showing everybody just how amazing. You told me I'm the tailor… I'm trying to put the suit together for you."

I hear the panic in my voice when I say this to Joe. "Charged with the task of showing everybody just how amazing…" I don't know what epithet to use to describe the sound of this sentence. Delusional? Self-absorbed? Histrionic? Who, exactly, am I imagining this *everybody* to be? But, epithets aside, in The Suit-writing days, that was my central obsession: How do I capture this man's story in a way that does it justice? *How*?

A favorite passage from Kafka's diary whispered in my ear the whole time I was writing that Suit, and still does: "This tremendous world I have inside my head. But how to free myself and free it without being torn to pieces? And a thousand times rather be torn to pieces than retain it in me or bury it. That, indeed, is why I am here, that is quite clear to me."[10] Applied purely to literary analysis, the passage sounds overblown and melodramatic, however much I happen to love it. In the context of writing Joe's story, though, it hits me with renewed power. Renewed urgency. There is, well, *anguish*, in the getting-of-things-right. There is *necessity*. Joe's story is in my hands.

I look at that emailed list of questions now, an artifact documenting my panic, and force myself to confront those asterisks beside #s 4 and 9. There, I see my own biases writ large. It's *action* I'm looking for, it seems. Blood and guts. There's a hungry quality to these questions:

***4) I want to know everything about that day that you stayed behind in the factory in the little ghetto. How exactly did you get out of the factory without them seeing you? Want to know every last detail about how you then got into the Gestapo headquarters. Everything. What did you see? What were people doing? What were they wearing? Where did you go once you opened the door? How long were you hiding there? What were you thinking about while you were hiding? What did your hiding space look like? How did you eventually get out of this building to join the workers returning? (This scene is going to be really, really important. Readers will be absolutely fascinated, so I want to make sure to set the stage as accurately as possible).

***9) Scenes of you fighting in the army. This one is going to be tough... but we absolutely need to see you here. And we need to know exactly what you were doing and feeling while you were fighting. Did you go directly into battle? Did you kill anyone? This is a HUGE piece of your story... what it means for you to be a soldier after your experience in the war. You've told me that you did things that you had to do because you were a soldier, things that you might not necessarily have done otherwise. We NEED to know what these things are, and we need to re-live them along with you.

It is exasperating, my insistence that there are parts of the story more worth telling than others, my assumption that my audience will agree about which parts these are. It's insulting, too, and arrogant, that I presume Joe would find it "tough" to relive his experience as a soldier. There's a near giddy quality to this second set of questions. I'm casting myself simultaneously as judge, jury and defense, hiding myself behind the royal we: "we NEED to know" all of these things that Joe might not have done otherwise, so that "we" can convict and exonerate him of these perceived crimes. There's urgency here, manufactured by the all caps. Only, I'm not sure where the urgency, this insistence that Joe must confront his demons in the presence of witnesses, is coming from.

But the recording captures the way Joe sidesteps my tactlessness. Of the numbered list he tells me:

"Listen, my son gave this list to me and says that you want to ask me these questions. So I read this several times already, but I didn't write anything about it, because it's not *talking*. It's better to take each one at a time. Because here you've got one thing and here you jump to something else, which is good because it's what you want to know. Am I right?"

"Yes," I tell him. "There's a few that, well they're all really important, but two areas that I think are the most important are, well not the most important..."

Almost imperceptibly, Joe says "ah," then waits for me to stick my foot in it deeper.

"... two areas that I think are the most important are when you're in Gestapo headquarters and when you are in the Israeli Army."

"They're *all* important. You think it's not important now, but it will be."

"Yes, I know. I know."

***

Why did I choose to end The Suit with Joe's refuge in the Jewish Brigade? Why *here*, when there are many moments in Joe's life that could serve as ending points? Or starting points, for that matter?

Among them:

• Joe's post-war life in Israel, from student of Hebrew to soldier in the War of Independence.[11]

• Joe's decision to come to the United States, pursuing the only connection he had: his uncle in Chicago, whose address he had seen just once on an envelope, memorized and kept in his mind as a kind of focal point during the gauntlet he'd been through.

• The moment of arrival itself in 1952, when Joe changes his name from Koenigheit to Koenig, streamlining his identity once and for all from "kingliness" to "king," from general principle to solitary actor.

• The moment when Joe meets his wife, giving her a bit of *schtick* that she saw through and gave right back, everything else fading around them as they decided that they were each what the other wanted.

• Joe's most recent near-death experience, a heart attack prompting him at last to tell his children his story.[12]

• Joe's return trip to Czestochowa in 2006—taken for the benefit of his daughter. He found Czestochowa every bit as inhospitable and hostile as he did when he left it in 1943 (the current inhabitants of his former apartment had ignored his knocks on the door, refusing him and his daughter entrance into the home that should still have been his).

Joe and I talked about all of these things over the course of our meetings. Any could have sufficed as endings or beginnings, happy and dismal among them. So why *here*?

Because that was the job: to construct a memoir of Joe's survival of the Holocaust. To chronicle his journey and collect the details of all that had been lost. There are conventions in Holocaust memoir, expectations, rules, assumptions. These are narratives tightly wrought, narratives that plunge readers into a seemingly alternative universe with a logic and landscape impossible for most to fathom. They provide snapshots of individuals clawing their way through this universe to come out on the other side. These are stories that deliver endings and hint at new beginnings. They are a testament to survival.

There is an essential claustrophobia to the genre, a narrowness of focus and concentration. They pinpoint. They do not sprawl.

My assignment was to stitch that Suit together with these assumptions in mind. This ending matches those assumptions. The end of the Holocaust is the end of the story, solidifying Joe's status as survivor, and pointing ahead to a future that looks like dawn breaking after a cold night. It isn't Wiesel or Levi or Frankl, but it does what it's supposed to do.

And I have to admit that I like the rhythm of that last paragraph. I like what it means to leave Joe in the quiet company of people who share a similar kind of pain. Safe, after so much brutality.

But remember this: In the telling of these tailored stories, choices—conscious, unconscious, poetic, prophetic—are made. They have to be. A necessary element of artifice in a genre that exists not only to preserve memory, but also to nail down truth.

***

So, Joe goes *into* Gestapo headquarters to hide? Doesn't this merit some obsessive attention? In the movie trailer playing endlessly in my mind, this scene is where it all begins, the money shot:

Joe, tiptoeing silently up the stairs.

No… wait… Joe, brazenly walking up the stairs.

Yes!

That's it: *Joe, hiding in plain sight.* I could hear the bellowing voice-over.

Because, when I'd read this part in the drafts I was given, and then in our follow-up conversations, there was one detail that I just kept coming back to.

"But how did you get *in* there?" I asked him.

"How did I get in there? Haven't you been listening? My dear, I walked through the front door."

Then he elaborated:

"I was in the lion's cage, I tell you. The lion's cage. If I had to do it now, I wouldn't do it. I'd be too afraid. But I did it then. I went in through the front door. *Nobody* goes into the Gestapo building—you have to be crazy. But, I'm telling you, when you have no choice and only one chance, you take it. *You take it.* Because, if you don't take it, you're dead."

There were moments that felt a bit like understatement in Joe's telling of things. His experience at Dachau, for example.

"So what can I tell you? Nothing much happened there," Joe leaned back in his chair, scratched his belly, and let out a theatrical yawn.

We'd hit the post-lunch slump. An unidentified mechanical humming floated over the boardroom. We were vaguely annoyed with it and with one another. I was pumping Joe for details. He was having none of it. It felt to me like passive aggression.

"I'm telling you," he said. "There's not a whole hell of a lot to tell."

This was *Dachau* we were talking about! Second only to Auschwitz in name recognition. Synonymous with all the chilling, nightmarish images etched in black and white in the pantheon of Holocaust remembrance. This was *it*? This was all he was going to give me?

"Listen," he said, sighing, resigned to parceling out a few more details if it meant I would change my line of questioning. "What can I tell you? It was horrible. Awful. We were so crowded into the bunks that we had to sleep sitting up, but there were four tiers of bunks, so there wasn't much room even for that. You were lucky if you could sit on the outer edge of the bunk, where there was more air. It was very tight. Very uncomfortable. You couldn't sleep. Not that you could sleep, anyway, because you didn't know what to expect, what might happen. You slept with your eyes open, so to speak."

"But, what did you do all day? Didn't you have to work?"

"No, we didn't have to do nothing. We were just sitting there all day long, like a bunch of morons. Or walking around, this and that. The guards didn't come to take us to work. Nothing. We could go in or out of our barracks when we wanted. It was strange. Totally disorganized."

"Did you talk with anyone? Hang out with anyone in particular?"

"Nah. It was everyone for himself. We kept to ourselves. You just did the best you could."

"But, well, did you see people getting killed? Were you afraid you would be killed?"

"No. Nothing like that. I didn't see nothing. Listen, everything was basically falling apart. The Germans knew they were losing the war. I didn't know it then, but the Germans were waiting for orders from the upper echelons of the Reich: every Jew in Dachau should be taken out and eliminated at once. Shot to death. They didn't want to leave any Jews alive."

"So, could you sense this at all? Did you feel this impending danger?"

"No. See, it was too late. The orders didn't come through until the last minute, and the American troops came sooner than they expected. They had no time to accomplish what they were told to do. A lot of Jewish people were in Dachau, and the Germans didn't have time to get rid of us all. That's it. Then one day, all of a sudden, there were no German guards around anymore. They had just disappeared, and the inmates were walking around with smiles on their faces—something I hadn't seen in years."

The stubborn literary urge in me to show the frantic pace of the last month—a race against the clock, the unremittingly hostile and horrifying conditions of two consecutive death marches, back-to-back encounters with two of the most unforgiving camps in the Nazi arsenal—was stymied by Joe's insistence that this was all rather anti-climactic. I was having trouble reconciling the graphic picture in my head with Joe's terse account.

But the way he tells it, it *was* something of an anti-climax, the last month before liberation. Or, at least, it wasn't the natural end of this story, which seems much more to be life after liberation. When he tells this part of the story, he hurries through it, utterly uninterested in belaboring the grisly details of this barbaric test of stamina and endurance. The images of death and carnage, of emaciated bodies frozen in poses of resignation, or anger, or despair, or hope-against-hope in the liberation that came a day, an hour, a moment too late—these are not the prevailing images of Joe's account. They're *there*, of course, as is his description of the people who died after liberation, their bodies rebelling against the C-rations distributed by the American soldiers, unaccustomed as they were to the heavy fat content after such meager provisions for so long. But much more revealing is the way he launches naturally into a philosophical meditation on what it takes to move on:

"You can cry to yourself and you can live with the memories, but you still have got to live a normal life; otherwise you're going to get sick. The way I see it, you've got two lives to live: the past and the present. But the thing is, you can't have two lives. You have to choose. Whatever happens, once it's over, it's over, and you've got to live for the future. Whatever steps you take now that you feel are right, they will affect your future. The future will prove whether you made the right decisions or not. You can't know whether it's going to be bad or good, but you've got to do the best you can in order to live a normal life. You want to live in as normal an environment as you can. That's the key."

***

Despite my insistence of its centrality, despite those panicked asterisks placed before Question #9 on the list, the scene I had imagined of Joe in the Israeli Army, sitting on a rooftop firing his rifle into the house below, didn't make the cut for The Suit. Though, originally, in my head, I was framing the story around Joe as a unified character moving, un-punctured, through history, at some point I decided that it was just cleaner (more concentrated, more linear, more conforming to the genre of Holocaust memoir) to end Joe's account where I did, in Italy with the Jewish Brigade. It was a literary and utilitarian choice. But it nags at me, the expected parameters of Holocaust memoir, the tension the genre imposes. Life-after-survival is not a standard component of these narratives, where survival is defined as being alive at the end of the war.

There is so much to Joe's life-after, so much that spills out beyond those parameters.

"You just go in there like a soldier, you hear what I'm telling you? Go in with your head up, walk like a soldier and you'll be okay. That's the key. Don't be afraid because you know you're right. Just do it. Remember that, that's the key to everything. Just do it. Don't be afraid. Head up, not down. Walk like a soldier."

Joe was giving me a pep-talk.

It was August 2009, and I had called Joe on the first day of class, in my usual state of first-day jitters, wanting to hear his voice. We hadn't met for months at this point, and I missed him. I missed his energy, his confidence, his ability to *deal*.

"I'm nervous, Joe." I told him. "I hate the first day. I always wish we could start on the second day, you know? When all the first impression stuff is over?" He didn't know the half of it. The painfully literal anxiety dreams that arrive, as if on cue, every semester the week before class starts: where I walk into a classroom with no syllabus, or forget what class it is I'm walking into, or forget altogether where it is I'm supposed to be. And then there are the real-time anxiety-producers: the awkward minutes before class begins, where we look at each other and wonder what to say. I usually crack lame jokes and call attention to the awkwardness, which does tend to defuse it. But the fear that first impressions can't be undone, the pressure of blowing it irreparably—I do carry that fear with me into every first encounter.

It's not a fear Joe seems to carry.

"You just do what I'm telling you, kid. You just do it and you'll be fine."

I did. I walked in there as I imagined a soldier would, as Joe described it. Head held high. Squashing my fear.

He was right, of course. I was fine.

Joe knew what he was talking about. He'd served two stints as a soldier: the first, in the Israeli Army during the War of Independence, the second, as an American soldier stationed in Trieste during the Korean War. He is fondly attached to both experiences and expresses an appreciation for their differences: Israel was the place that brought him back to life, the War of Independence an opportunity for him to show his pride in and full support for the Zionist dream; Trieste was an extended bachelor party ("I drank a lot of beer and fooled around with women, and that's the way I spent my army duty"). All the same, he sees continuity in these experiences, and between his life as a soldier and his life as a survivor. We'd talked about it once:

"To me, there's so much wrapped up in understanding you as a soldier," I hear myself say on the recording. "Because, that's *you*, right? Your story doesn't end with the Holocaust... in some ways it begins there. If we can understand you as a soldier, it helps us to understand how you got through it all. Because you were the same person, right?"

"Yes, yes I was," he answered. "Okay, you want to do it, baby? You want to do it? Okay! Let's do it!" More animated than I ever saw him. He pushed his chair away from the boardroom table, the casters propelling him a foot or so. He clapped his hands together.

"So here's what it is. To be a soldier, a real soldier, you have to follow orders. If you follow orders, you are a good soldier. So be proud of yourself, number one. Number two, by doing what you're told to do, sometimes you don't like to do it, but you HAVE to do it, that's why you're a soldier. A soldier is a soldier, no matter what. But you see, there are two types of soldiers: some who listen and some who think it's just a play. It's *not* just a play, it's life or death.

So, listen. You get an order to shoot, you better shoot, otherwise someone else is going to shoot at you. So the Commander tells you, 'just shoot them and don't ask questions,' that's exactly what you do. Because, otherwise they'll shoot you. You're a dead duck if you don't. So I did it. I don't know if I killed anybody or not. I assume that I did. But that's not important. What's important is that I did what I had to do. And that's about all I can tell you about being a soldier. You just do it, because you know you want to live. If he's coming at you with a gun, what are you going to do? Tell him, 'come on in, take a cup of coffee?' NO. No way. What I know is that I did what I had to do and I came out alive."

I was stuck on something as I listened to him.

"I'm confused here, Joe. I mean, you talk about how being a good soldier means recognizing that you're part of a larger unit, that you're never alone. Isn't this the exact opposite approach you needed to take to get you through the Holocaust? I mean you were completely and totally alone then."

"No," Joe said. "It's the same thing. You see, then I was the commander, my own commander. You don't have anybody telling you what to do. You have to take the bull by the horns, you either live or die."

I didn't get how this could be the same thing.

"It's just that the person that you seem to be when you're making your way through all of those camps, well, you didn't seem like a person who would want to take orders from anybody. So I find it really interesting that you're so committed to being a soldier."

"Well, that's a different story. If everybody wanted to be the commander, there'd be no soldiers, just assholes. You see, there's a time and a place for being a commander and a time and a place for being a soldier."

I still didn't quite get it, but loved the shape of his thoughts.

I picked up my coffee, which I kept refilling, more to keep warm than anything else, took a sip, then went for it:

"Okay, Joe. So here's a really weird question."

"Let me have it," he said, enjoying every bit of this.

"Well, okay. In the normal world..."

"Normal is my middle name," he interrupted, chuckling.

"In the normal world, what position should you take, soldier or commander?"

Joe looked at me in such a way to confirm that my question was, indeed, weird.

And then he spoke slowly, carefully, as if handing over a secret password that couldn't afford to be misunderstood:

"The guy who gives the orders is supposed to know what to do. You as a soldier, you don't tell him what to do. You've got to follow orders. Good or bad, there is only the one commander. But if, on the other side we've got a commander who doesn't know what to do, and he's afraid or whatever, if he's in battle, he would lose half of his people. This happens all the time, people die because the commander doesn't know what he's doing."

Try as I might, I couldn't grasp what he was telling me. There seemed to me an unspoken prescription in this, an implied course of action for the second scenario he had outlined. Mutiny, perhaps? But then why didn't he just say so?

"Okay, so now you're not in war, there's a different kind of world you're living in. You're just living your life. Do you think about whether or not you have to live according to these rules of taking or giving orders? Do you think like a soldier?"

"Well, I don't know, I guess I let the commander take care of me."

I pointed up, starting to get it. "Is that the commander?"

"Yep, that's right."

Not mutiny, exactly. But not exactly not-mutiny either.

***

Joe both recognizes and doesn't recognize the literary potential of his story. That is, he both sees and doesn't see his experience as a "story" worth telling, a narrative. The conflicting drives to remember and to move on pull at Joe, competing for dominance.

"When I came to this country, okay, I decided, I'm going to live a normal life," he once said to me. "I'm going to go to work, to school. I'll get married. I'll get a job. Live a regular life. And I won't tell my kids what I did, what I was. My kids didn't know anything about me. But there comes a time where you have to do it, because if you keep it to yourself it will kill you. So now my kids know, but I'm not telling them every day. I'm not always reminding them. I don't want my kids to be sick. I don't want them to feel sorry for me. That's no good, because then they won't be able to live normal."

These terms—*normal, sick*—nagged at me. I felt judged by them in a way I hadn't expected, which probably had something to do with my father, who couldn't be called normal by any stretch of the imagination, let alone by the conventional markers Joe used to describe a "normal life… a regular life." Maybe it was the way Joe opposed sickness and normalcy to one another—it caught me off guard. If pushed to present my own poles of opposition, I would have said sickness and health. Sickness, in this case, would still be the condition you'd want to avoid, if given the option, but it wouldn't be cast as an aberration. It would just be an unfortunate circumstance, something to be treated, perhaps pitied.

I want clearer definitions from him, even if they clarify the judgment. What is normal? What is sick? How can categories like this still apply in the context of a world that so thoroughly ripped them apart?

"Look, I'll be honest," he says, his already heavy Polish accent growing somehow heavier over the course of his explanation. "I know a lot of people, you know, who survived the camps. They dwell on it and dwell on it. What the hell is going on with these people? 'Here,' I want to say to them, 'you're here, you're alive, you've got love, you've got a family. What the hell? Live with it.' Look, look at my children. They're not crying because I was in the camp. You look at it. They're all normal.

They know I was in the Holocaust. That's it. They know. I don't want them to feel sorry for me. It's not their fault, it's not my fault. It happened that I was born at that time, in that place. And I had to suffer for losing my family at a young time, and that's the story."

He was shaking his head now, so vehemently opposed he was to the possibility that he should dwell on his experience. And yet, here we were, writing this memoir, dwelling.

"Never, never will I do it," he insisted. "A lot of them, you know, the people in the camps, they still live with it, with what happened, with what was. But I said, 'No, I don't do that. I don't tell what was. I don't live in what was. I know what I did, I know what happened. I have to live with it, but I'm not going to cry in public. And my kids— each one of them—has a healthy mind. They do what they want to do. They don't cry. And I think that's how it should be. Am I right or am I wrong? You tell me, you be the judge."

Me? The judge? Good god, I hope not. I would so much rather feel judged by Joe, as I did a minute ago, than judge him. It seems to me that Joe earned the right to judge by virtue of the unparalleled shit he went through. In comparison to all that, my cushy suburban upbringing and "coming of age" in the happy oblivion of the 80s pretty much disqualifies me from judging Joe's actions or opinions. Not to mention that I *do* cry all the time in public, which renders me a biased judge at the very least.

But, judgment and moratoria on crying in public completely aside, I was curious. As resistant as he is to dwelling, why does Joe want to tell his story? So I asked him, point blank: "Why, Joe? Why do you want people to know? Why are we doing this?"

Who is this for?

***

That glossy-covered paperback, containing The Suit and bearing my name, was a kind of betrayal.

Joe's family got the book they wanted. And they wanted others to have it, so they printed untold copies, changed chapter titles, made edits, put my name on the cover and sold them at the Illinois Holocaust Museum in Skokie without my knowledge. I only found out about it when a cousin of Joe's emailed me, in 2013, asking if I could send her a copy. They'd run out, apparently, at the Museum.

In the fall of 2015, I called the Museum and purchased a copy of my own. I paid full price. Fifteen dollars, plus shipping. Joe's family titled it *I Choose Life: Memories of a Holocaust Survivor Joseph Koenig.* On the back, there is a synopsis:

> *I Choose Life* is a book of memories. [...] Joe's story is one of endurance, perseverance and a will to survive. His memoir is a true testament to the human spirit. Joe was continuously faced with life and death decisions. Joe's courage, strength and unwavering determination sustained him through the barbaric treatment he suffered during the reign of Nazi terror. Throughout those horrific days, Joe Chose Life!

I'm angry when I read this. Not because the understanding Joe's family and I had come to (that I would give them a family version of the story for their own private use while I pursued the story that hadn't yet been told) had been broken. I recognize how blurry public/private lines become in the midst of memoir, just as I recognize the family's eagerness to share Joe's story with others. I share it, too.

No. I'm angry at the violent anonymity of this description. At the way Joe is effectively erased by these lines that could have been written about any survivor.

This was the heart-sinking feeling I had had at the table when Joe's son handed me that memoir. This was it exactly.

The book bears—some solace—a dedication from Joe:

This book is dedicated to my loving wife,
Children and grandchildren
Who wanted to know my story.
And to all of the victims of the Holocaust
Whose stories will remain untold

And an epigraph, a poem by Ida Scott Taylor, "One Day at a Time":

One day at a time—this is enough
Do not look back and grieve over the past, for it is gone;
And do not be troubled about the future,
For it has not yet come.

Live in the present, and make it so beautiful
That it will be worth remembering.

The version that I had given to the family had had a different epigraph, a passage from the *Dhammapada*, the sayings of the Buddha.

Live in joy,
In health,
Even among the afflicted.

Live in joy,
In peace,
Even among the troubled.

The Taylor poem retains something of the spirit of what I was going for in my epigraph. It doesn't really matter, they both now feel sentimental to me, overbearingly prescriptive. Epigraphs in general run that risk. They presume that we won't know what to do with the contents of a book if the framework isn't announced—however cryptically or explicitly—on that first page. I knew the kind of book Joe's family wanted would have an epigraph, and, so, I gave them one.

Who is The Suit for? Joe's family. And Joe. Of course it is.

So maybe I'm imposing a scope and sense of project on something that was never mine to impose upon. Maybe my anger is unreasonable. Maybe I'm just wrong to be thinking about the whole thing as an either-or—as in, glossy paperback *or* my not-yet-found-form. Because, there's this indisputable fact: on the paperback's back cover is a picture of Joe, standing at the water's edge of the Fountain of the Righteous outside the Illinois Holocaust Museum in Skokie. His grin is wider, more sincere, than in any other picture contained in the book. Hands in pockets, squinting a bit at the sun's glare, slightly off-center of the memorial plaques stretching out in both directions behind him, he looks at ease in this space that has become for him something like a second home. At the time the picture was taken, he was serving as a docent for the museum, telling his story to scores and scores of visitors, catching them off-guard with his sometimes-brash humor, hugging nearly every one. He was also attending a workshop, hosted by the museum, for local survivors to write their stories in their own words.

And there's also this: the front cover of my copy of the paperback boasts a round, gold "Autograph Copy" sticker. Joe's signature is on the title page.

It's fair to say, then, that this version made Joe happy. He never told me so. We didn't have the chance to have that conversation. But I have to imagine him happy in this place so dear to him, signing copies of this concrete thing in the world, grinning that toothy grin as he hands them over, one by one, to people whose lives he has touched.

Buttons Jut Out

Joe has swagger. He had it before the war, he had it during the war, and he has it now when he tells me stories like the one about his hiding in Gestapo headquarters.

To be clear, swagger is *not* chutzpah.

Chutzpah is something others give to you, a quality or trait people assign to you that they find both admirable and annoying. A mix of nervy and courageous, it suggests that you've overstepped your designated place, you've gone beyond where you're supposed to go. When people describe those to whom they've assigned this trait, they usually do so with an alternating chuckle and sense of indignation. Depending on the degree of overstepping, the chuckle may get louder and what may start as a hint of judgment may become outright condemnation. But both parts have to be represented (even if unequally) for it to be chutzpah. For it to be chutzpah, we have to be laughing while we wag our fingers.

For instance: my dad was basically an (unsuccessful) career criminal who stole thousands and thousands of dollars and merchandise from just about every place he worked during his life (including the family business—my grandfather's shop—on my mother's side).

He also taught a course in business ethics at a Junior college in Philly.

That's chutzpah.

Swagger, by contrast, is something no one else can give you. You have it or you don't. When you have swagger, you create your own boundaries; by definition there is no overstepping them because they move with you, shifting with your own choices and decisions. There is no yardstick by which to measure it, no way that judgment can come anywhere near it. To the contrary, when we see people who have swagger, we feel our own limitations, our own cowardice. We recognize that our actions have less to do with ingenuity than they do efficiency or ritual or habit. And those who have swagger don't particularly care about how others would judge them, even if they could. They exist in a space of pure possibility, beyond any petty labels like right and wrong.

***

Have I communicated Joe's swagger effectively in The Suit I have crafted? I'm not sure. It waxes and wanes. For instance, there's one section that grates on me. I cringe when I read it:

> *But try as he might, his thoughts kept drifting back to all he had already lost. He and his father had been away at a nearby work camp—his father, who spoke perfect German, was chosen to serve as foreman—when his mother and two sisters were taken away to Treblinka. Rumors of gas chambers circulated through the ghetto, but Joe had no way of knowing for sure that this was the fate they had met. Sitting here, now, he contemplated the possibility that he would never see them again. He tried not to think of all the things he might have said the last time he saw them, had he known it was the last time. Tried not to think about the playful arguments he'd always had with his sisters in the time "before." It hurt him deeply to remember this life, the nurturing home his mother created, filled with love and laughter, awash in the happy din of the radio and phonographs playing—it seemed perpetually—in the background. Theirs had been a typical Jewish home—observant, but not particularly religious. In this cramped closet, Joe remembered the smell of the warm challah his mother baked every Friday. When they returned from synagogue, she would light candles in the sparkling silver candlesticks, and Joe's father would say Kiddush over the wine. He remembered, with a sharp pang, the makeshift Bar Mitzvah his parents had managed to organize for him, in a neighbor's apartment, just after the war started. There had been no more temples to go to, then, but they had managed to cobble together a minyan to see their son become an adult in the eyes of tradition.*
>
> *He was an adult now, so it seemed, but he was really still a child. A scared and hungry fourteen year old, huddled and alone in this place he had somehow found to protect him. Before he could stop it from coming, a collapsed moment, the symbol for him of a happier time, came into his thoughts: the bicycle that his father had bought for him, out of the blue on a summer day the year before the Germans had invaded Poland. His father had taken him to the bicycle shop and told him to pick one out. The one he chose was midnight blue, with light-colored, unpainted wooden rims bent forward like rams' horns. A racing bike. Joe rode it everywhere his parents would let him, and, when he returned home, would lovingly clean it and oil the gears and pedals, the ritual preserving what felt like freedom to him.*

A year later, Joe received a notice to bring the bicycle to a local warehouse. He didn't know why. It turned out that the Polish army needed all bicycles for the soldiers' transportation. With tears in his eyes, Joe stood in line, waiting to hand over the bike to a civilian, who tried to comfort him as he took the bike from Joe. As he walked away, Joe glanced back over his shoulder for one last look at his bike, which had now joined many, many others, all lined up next to each other, each with a promissory note, with the names and addresses of the children and adults who would never see them again.

It was just a bike, but it somehow became for him everything that was gone. He wrapped himself now in the pain of all of these memories, dreading to remember, dreading more to forget.

I wrote this at the request of Joe's sons, who wanted me to include more details about Joe's family and life before the war. The bike was a memory they'd heard a lot about, with particular emphasis on the fact that it was midnight blue. The challah was, too, as was the makeshift Bar Mitzvah. I decided to go all out, wrapping it all together, piling memory upon memory, laying it on extra thick.

The first draft I'd written went like this:

He stepped gingerly onto the first stair, testing it for creaks that might give him away. Hearing none, he bolted up one flight of stairs and then another and another. The stairs ended here, and gave way to a room—empty—where he stopped. A storage space, it looked like it hadn't been used for some time. Joe relaxed. Finding a corner that would hide him from the line of vision—if someone were to come unexpectedly through the door—he sat huddled there for hours, intermittently napping and nursing what had become a more persistent ache in his stomach and head. In the empty room, he tried not to hear his own thoughts, tried not to think about how alone he was. Tried not to think or feel at all.

Evening eventually came, and with it the much-too-early dark of January. Shaking himself out of the sleepy fog of those hours, Joe realized that he'd have to make his way back out now if he wanted to blend back in with the workers that had left that morning. It seemed years since he had seen his father, decades since he had taken the advice his father had given him in the hopes of protecting him, the last remaining shred of what a father could do for a son in this absurd world.

He just wanted to hug him now, to hold on to him.

I wanted to leave Joe huddled there, in that rhythmic movement of willed oblivion, alone in that hiding space he'd risked so much to find. I wanted to keep him insulated by an absolute silence that might—just maybe—make his head and stomach stop hurting.

Retroactive healing, as it were.

What bugs me so much about my altered version is the noisiness—the *nosiness*—of it all. The intrusiveness.

Because, after all, the version of the story Joe told me *was* quiet. It was emptied out of memories, of any conscious thought process. It was entirely visceral. When he sat there in that hiding space, his head throbbed, his stomach ached and he fell in and out of sleep, edges blurred to waking. He was master over the thoughts and feelings he willed not to intrude. The version I gave his family shows him caving in, succumbing to a force greater than his own will. And it feels to me a betrayal. As I parry these versions against one another I recall Tim O'Brien's words: "In any war story, but especially a true one, it's difficult to separate what happened from what seemed to happen... The pictures get jumbled; you tend to miss a lot. And then afterward, when you go to tell about it, there is always that surreal seemingness, which makes the story seem untrue, but which in fact represents the hard and exact truth as it *seemed*."[13] Joe's version is the hard and exact truth, its seemingness devoid of nostalgia or reflection.

As I look again at my original attempt to capture that seemingness, I see the seeds of what became the family version. I see the urge, in both versions, to narrow the sphere of what took place in that storage space. In the original version, it narrowed in the direction of Joe's father, culminating in that wished-for hug. The second version contains his sons' impulse to wrap him in memories of his family and lost possessions. Both versions came from a similar desire to comfort Joe.

But such are the dangers of storytelling, of telling a *true* story: neither the family version nor my original is more demonstrably true. Both violate Joe's hard and exact truth, even (and perhaps especially) in the midst of good intentions.

"Why are we doing this? *Why??*" I asked.

Joe hurled my question back at me, looking at me with uncontained astonishment.

"Why tell this story? Why not? Let them know, it's important. There will be a time when there won't be any more people who can tell anybody else. To make sure it doesn't happen again. Never, ever, ever again. I'm doing this for my family, and so my family can read it and say to their children: 'We have to let people know what happened, generation to generation.'"

Primo Levi flashes across my mind, who writes in his preface to *Survival in Auschwitz*: "The need to tell our story to 'the rest,' to make 'the rest' participate in it, had taken on for us, before our liberation and after, the character of an immediate and violent impulse, to the point of competing with our other elementary needs."[14]

Joe was leaning heavily on his elbows, balancing his sitting weight on the table in front of him. He thrust his hands out and grabbed mine, pulling them toward him across the table. Our clasped hands knocked over my nearly empty coffee cup. A milky stream fanned out thinly between us.

"Listen to me, okay?" he implored, a palpable urgency in his usually measured voice. An immediate and violent impulse. "We *have* to tell this story, okay, because you have to see what people do to other people. You've got to make sure that this doesn't come back again and kill your children and your children's children. You never know what tomorrow brings. God forbid this happens in this country. We have to come out and talk about it. That's why people write books. I know it, because I lived it. You didn't, so how would you know? That's why I feel that I should do it. Listen, we've got plenty of time to tell this thing. Guts keep me in good shape. We'll do this, don't you worry. Here's the way it is: you're here—we're all here—for a visit. Just do good things and take advantage of being here. If you don't, you're a son-of-a-bitch and no one gives a shit about you."

***

Of course Joe's sons are right that the information about the bike, the challah, the Bar Mitzvah should be included in a story of Joe's survival. Of course these details help to flesh out who Joe is, where he comes from, what he cares about, what he lost. Of course his children feel connected to these images that announce the specificity of Joe's experience, that make up their family tapestry.

In my conversation with Joe's sons, it was clear that, to them, it didn't really matter where or how this information was included, just *that* it was. I was the one who made the decision to clutter up that hiding space with these memories, not them.

Still, I'm left to wonder how to tell these kinds of stories when the intended audience is "the rest." *Is* there a way to write a section about a midnight blue racing bike, challah, and a makeshift Bar Mitzvah that makes others participate and feel the stakes at the same time that it satisfies the survivor's visceral need to tell his or her story?

***

Elie Wiesel's *Night* is generally held up as the *sine qua non* of Holocaust memoirs. The standard bearer of the genre. The blurb on the front cover of my copy reads:

"A SLIM VOLUME OF TERRIFYING POWER"
—THE NEW YORK TIMES

Normally one to resist popular opinion, I have to agree with this assessment. The book was like a gut punch the first time I read it, and I still can't read passages out loud (as I've tried to do, in classes or conferences) without breaking down. The gravity of the text lies in its leanness, in all that isn't said. It does bear mention, though, that it took a monumental feat of editing to get to this slim volume. The stripped down 100-page manuscript the world now knows as *Night* originally weighed in at over 800 pages.

Wiesel's style in the published version is terse, unsparing, brutal, and extraordinarily lyrical. He makes heavy use of the white space on the page. Silence embeds his narrative.

> *Night. No one prayed, so that the night would pass quickly. The stars were only sparks of the fire which devoured us. Should that fire die out one day, there would be nothing left in the sky but dead stars, dead eyes.*
> *There was nothing else to do but to get into bed, into the beds of the absent ones; to rest, to gather one's strength.*
>
> *Never shall I forget that night, the first night in camp, which has turned my life into one long night, seven times cursed and seven times sealed. Never shall I forget that smoke. Never shall I forget the little faces of the children, whose bodies I saw turned into wreaths of smoke beneath a silent blue sky.*
> *Never shall I forget those flames which consumed my faith forever.*
> *Never shall I forget that nocturnal silence which deprived me, for all eternity, of the desire to live. Never shall I forget those moments which murdered my God and my soul and turned my dreams to dust. Never shall I forget these things, even if I am condemned to live as long as God Himself. Never.*[15]

83

These are iconic passages, signaling to readers the expansive symbolism of his chosen title. Steeped in negation, shrouded in absence. No
other word will do. *Night.*

The babysitter looked at me without a flicker of recognition when I told her what I was working on one day.

"He's a Holocaust survivor," I told her. "I'm writing his story."

"Holocaust?" She asked, pulling her heavy brown ponytail over her shoulder. "What's that? I've never heard of it."

She looked so young to me at that moment, though I was only six and a half years older. I stumbled around for a quick explanation.

"It's, well, you know, it happened during World War Two, in Europe, the Germans murdered six million Jews. Millions of other people were murdered, too, but the Jews were murdered just because they were Jews."

This was perhaps the least nuanced explanation ever. I tried not to picture the disgusted faces of my colleagues in the History department.

"You've really never heard of this? You didn't study this in school or anything?" I was having trouble looking her in the eye, conscious all of a sudden of the cultural chasm between us. I went to the bookshelf and found what I was looking for: my well-worn copy of *Night*. I handed it to her.

"Here, if you're interested—not that I'm saying you should be interested—this book is really, really good. It's probably the most famous book about the Holocaust."

And then I left for work, quickly, afraid that if I didn't, one of two things would happen: I'd start crying or I'd start lecturing. I wasn't sure which was worse.

I sat in my car in the driveway for a while, shaking a little bit, trying to sort out what I was thinking and feeling and why any of it mattered. I couldn't wrap my head around it: a thirty-one year-old American woman who didn't know anything about the Holocaust. A woman who lives for her kids and her church. The kind and sensitive person who took wonderful care of my sons. How could she not know about this?

I tried a more self-reflective approach. Why did I care whether or not she knew about the Holocaust? Me, the person who frequently refers to herself as a self-hating Jew? Who refuses to go to the camps and who gives unsolicited opinions about how the Holocaust should or should not be represented? Who feels a kind of pathological guilt for obsessing over this particular example of how humans destroy each other, when there are so many other possible examples to choose from?

Why did I need her to know? And what was it that I was expecting to come of her knowing?

A line from a T.S Eliot poem came unannounced into my head: "After such knowledge, what forgiveness?" The line haunted me all day.

"I read it," she told me two days later. "I mean, I read most of it. I didn't really have enough time to read the whole book, but I read what I could while the kids were napping."

"What did you think?" I asked.

"It's horrible, it's just horrible. I can't believe people can do this to other people. I can't believe this wasn't that long ago. How can people treat people like this?"

"I know. I know. I don't know."

I don't know.

***

It was the absence, the negation, the silence of *Night* I kept hearing in my head when I compiled that list of questions for Joe and set about the writing of The Suit. It was this silence I heard overtaking that storage space, and that persistent "never"—an existential protest fueling Joe's astounding creativity in discerning how to transform danger into protection. Stylistically, the silence matches the way Joe generally tells his story, without embellishment. But much as Wiesel's style serves as a model for The Suit, there is an important distinction to be made between his use of the term "never"—the driving force behind the mantra of Holocaust remembrance—and Joe's bristling at the getting stuck, the unhealthy dwelling, that a literal interpretation of "never forget" might promote. Where Wiesel's "never" encompasses the unthinkable to Joe—"which deprived me, for all eternity, of the desire to live"—Joe's "never" is life affirmation, refusal to see limitation, rejection of constraints. His "never" is a battle-cry, an assertion of freedom. There is lightness to his "never," fluidity, motion, humor.

Swagger.

***

"Do you really need to use those bad words there, Beth?" Joe's wife asked me. "I mean, it doesn't have to be so dirty does it? Kids might be reading this."

It was October 2009. We were sitting in a Corner Bakery near Skokie—Joe, his wife, his son, and me—going over the draft of the story I'd written and distributed to the family. The scent of fresh bread, mixed with cinnamon and coffee, hung over the table. We were stuck on a section I'd named "Joe Boxer" in the version I'd given them. They found it problematic:

> *"Are you Jewish?" some of the more vicious [tough guys] asked Joe one day.*
>
> *"No," he answered. "Why would you ask that?"*
>
> *Shit, he thought. This was bad.*
>
> *"Because we think you are. You look like a Jew. You smell like a Jew."*
>
> *They gathered around him now, right up in his face.*
>
> *Joe let loose a string of creative and complicated obscenities in Polish. This should have ended the discussion. In Yiddish, maybe, a Jew would talk like this. But not Polish. It just wasn't done.*
>
> *They still weren't convinced.*
>
> *"I don't care how well you speak Polish," one guy insisted, "I think you're a dirty, stinking Jew." He shoved Joe.*
>
> *Joe shoved him back.*
>
> *"What you think and what I say are two different things."*
>
> *"So what?"*
>
> *"So, you bastard," Joe went on, trying to put him on the defensive. "So you must have done something wrong if you're in here."*
>
> *"Yeah, well let's just see." The group moved closer, menacing now. "Let's go to the washroom. You pull your pants down, we'll see who's a Jew, clear as day."*
>
> *"Why don't you pull your pants down, you bunch of jackasses. The only ones I'll pull my pants down for are the Germans. Who the hell do you people think you are? You go to hell!"*

Joe was completely bluffing now, remembering how his cousin, a boxer, would puff himself up during a fight and imitating him as best he could. He weaved and bobbed, deflecting the taunts as if they were blows.

I loved writing this scene. Loved how, in writing it, through Joe, I got to threaten to beat the shit out of those bullies. Love how Joe is preserved here in all his underdog bravado, never needing to make good on his impossible threats and taunts. He's badass here. Swagger personified. For good measure, I added a "bastard" here, a "jackass" there, and lingered over Joe's description of the Polish curses he hurled to convince them he wasn't Jewish.

But it wasn't just me who loved it. The day Joe described this to me, his eyes lit up, he spoke more quickly, he bobbed-and-weaved in his chair, as if his muscle memory had kicked in. He was back in the moment, back in the fight, reliving this close call. Owning his narrow escape with pride.

"Yes," Joe's son agreed, "I don't know about this part. I don't like the way my father comes across, with all this cursing. Like, here, in this line:

'*Shit*, he thought. This was bad.'

What if you just took out the 'shit' and said: 'This was bad,' he thought.'"

"Yes, that would be better," Joe's wife confirmed. "It really doesn't have to be dirty to get the point across. I think maybe this whole section is too vulgar, there's too much obscenity, too much violence. It just looks... bad."

"Joe's on the verge of having the crap beaten out of him by a bunch of hardened criminals. I think 'shit' captures it pretty well." I was having trouble keeping the frustration out of my voice. It made no sense to me, this basic aversion to obscenity. My father had taught me at an early age how powerful a well-placed curse could be. He cursed as easily as he breathed, so much so that it never seemed obscene to me. Just colorful. Just real.

I was also remembering, conveniently, a passage from Viktor Frankl's, *Man's Search for Meaning.* Soon after arriving in Auschwitz, Frankl shows a fellow prisoner a manuscript he's been working on, his "life's work," hidden in his pocket. He implores him to understand that he must keep it at all costs. The prisoner's reaction? "A grin spread slowly over his face, first piteous, then more amused, mocking, insulting, until he bellowed one word at me in answer to my question, a word that was ever present in the vocabulary of the camp inmates: 'Shit!'"[16]

I rest my case.

I locked eyes with Joe. He had been silent this whole time. He looked back and forth at us with a vaguely amused grin on his face, the aftermath of storytelling spilling out before him. Now he looked directly at me, vague grin turning into open, toothy smile, encouraging me to go on.

I rallied.

"I'm sorry, but I don't understand why you think it's dirty, or why you think anyone would have a hard time accepting that, in the midst of all this, Joe's going to get pissed and let a few curses fly. Who wouldn't? I mean, Jesus, he's lost everyone, everything. 'Shit' is an understatement, don't you think? But besides all that, this is how Joe described the scene to me. These are *his* words. If this is what he's thinking, why shouldn't people know that?"

And then, joining Frankl, O'Brien—again—in the back of my head: "A true war story is never moral. It does not instruct, nor encourage virtue, nor suggest models of proper human behavior, nor restrain men from doing the things men have always done [...] You can tell a true war story by its absolute and uncompromising allegiance to obscenity and evil... You can tell a true war story if it embarrasses you. If you don't care for obscenity, you don't care for truth [...]"[17]

Hearing O'Brien, I threw down the gauntlet of righteous indignation: truth or fiction? What do you want to stand behind? Kind of a cheap shot on my part, but I felt protective of this scene in a way I didn't want to have to explain.

As far as Joe was concerned, I didn't have to.

"Keep it there," he said. "I want it like this."[18]

***

But I rushed away too quickly from Joe's description of his partici-
pation in the War of Independence, from his statement: "I don't know
if I killed anybody or not. I assume that I did. But that's not important.
What's important is that I did what I had to do".

The conversation played out slowly. For at least an hour on one of
our visits, Joe talked to me about his life as an Israeli soldier, in more
detail and with more deliberate lessons than any other part of his story.
The mysterious line of reasoning about the commander that I described
earlier? That was just an interlude tying together several raw descriptions of battle.

Which was really rather a stretch for me to envision, given my limited—non-existent—experience with war. Disproving the teacherly
mantra, "there are no stupid questions," I asked Joe, "Can you tell me
what kind of warfare it was? I mean, I know in World War I and II there
was trench warfare. So, like logistically? What was happening? What
was the battleground like?"

"It was like I told you," Joe said impatiently. "See, there was a small
house, and we had to eliminate it, otherwise the Arabs would have tak-
en it and killed us. So, we had to save it. There were a few of us guys on
the roof who were shooting into it, you know. Whether we killed somebody or not, I don't know. I didn't look. The strongest I can say is this:
when I was shooting, I know I did okay. Whether I killed someone, I
don't know, and I cared less."

"So, strategically, they were there and they had lain claim to this
house? So you were trying to get it?" Really trying to *see* it, the situation
that would prompt what might be called morbid indifference in any
other case.

"That's right. We were on top, we had the advantage."

"So, you were on top, shooting into the roof of the house," I said,
parroting him. "Can you remember, when it was going on, was there
any conversation with your fellow soldiers, any shouting going on?"

When I listen to the recordings now, I hear Joe sigh, then say, "Listen, we all had the same job to do. We were told to eliminate that house. Because it was in our view, you know. So we had to eliminate that house, and to eliminate the Arabs from there. And I assume that we did."

Joe's dismissal of the importance of whether or not he killed anybody introduced a crack in the foundation, the possibility of moral relativism in a landscape that had always been presented to me as defiantly absolute. How could it not be important? But, despite the shrill, pedantic voice that announced itself—uninvited—inside my head when Joe told me this, I kept pushing for more details, more scenes, fascinated.

So he gave me more.

"I was under fire too, you know. I had to be careful. We were in Jaffa, next to Tel Aviv. The Arabs were there on that side and they were shooting at us and we were here on this side, and here is an open place—one end were the Arabs, the other end were the Jews and in the middle was nobody."

Joe was drawing the battle scene on a napkin with a pen, scratching holes in the flimsy paper as the ink threatened to run out. X's for Arabs, O's for Jews, hash marks for the wall of fire in between.

"We were shooting at them, they were shooting at us. The objective is to kill them. We wanted to clear this place right here and take it."

Joe circled a spot near the line of X's. A sketch that left little room for interpretation.

"We didn't have much to shoot with. So, in order to let the Arabs think that we had a lot of ammunition, what we did was we used the same gun from this side and then the other guy took the rifle from me and shot it from over here. You know, we only had one rifle, but each guy shot it."

"Wow," I said. "Wow, that's really intense."

"Yes, it was. And that's about it, that's about all I can tell you."

"So what happened when the war was over?"

Joe shrugged and answered, "So we get orders to abandon, so we go. Or, to give more fire. To kill them and get them away. That's it."

Tim O'Brien wrote: "In a true war story, if there's a moral at all, it's like the thread that makes the cloth. You can't tease it out. You can't extract the meaning without unraveling the deeper meaning. And, in the end, really, there's nothing much to say about a true war story, except maybe 'Oh.'"[19]

Or maybe "Wow," in my case.

I could have listened to Joe's war stories all day, elbows on the table, head cupped in hand, follow-up questions dissolving into inanities. It was the element of pure strength in all of it, the way this chapter of his life wiped away any traces of victim status. I loved the power of the role he'd stepped into, and *that* he'd stepped into a role of power. Recalling a piece of Joe's experience in Rakow, I started to understand how, for him, there could be continuity between his life as a prisoner and his life as a soldier:

> *Eden was a bastard, but he was also rather predictable. At least, his schedule was, and Joe had him figured out pretty quickly. As long as he appeared to be working when Eden was around, there was no problem. So Joe did this, masterfully engaged in his own performance. Pretty soon, Joe was watching Eden more than Eden was watching him, turning the tables on this man who remained oblivious to his shrinking sphere of control. Joe carried a broom with him at all times, sweeping furiously when he saw Eden, and resting as soon as his eyes were turned. He soon discovered that he could disappear behind a machine or into a corner, or, even better, that he could hide away for longer. Always exhausted from the grueling ritual and meager provisions of the camp, Joe learned when Eden would be away at lunch or a meeting, and then he would nap in the broom closet, which he locked from the inside. Or, he slipped into the restroom, where he napped—sitting on a toilet—before washing up as best as he could in the sink, drying himself with the old newspaper placed there for this purpose.*
>
> *Joe played it perfectly, timing his emergence from the closet or restroom carefully to coincide with Eden's return.*
>
> *Eden never caught on.*

Joe and I talked about this scene on one of our visits, just after he'd finished describing to me his father's death. A nearly aerobic transition, the air and energy seemed to come back into the boardroom when Eden came up. A good thing. We both needed to breathe.

"I think it's kind of cool that his name was Eden. I mean, there's such great symbolic potential here, don't you think?"

Joe raised his eyebrow, more than skeptical, dismissing my literary tic. "I don't care. Symbolism? I don't care."

"Well, anyway," I told him, "I love that you, kind of, you're one step ahead of him. You know that whenever he can catch people not working, he gives them hell. So you watched him watching you."

He laughed, proud.

"And then, all of a sudden, you're resting."

He laughed again, remembering. "That's right."

"How did you manage to do that and still get your work done?" Now I laughed, just as proudly.

"I took the broom... and pretended..." he mimed the action, hand-caught-in-the-cookie-jar grinning.

"It sounds like you managed to find some time to get some rest."

"I *always* found something, believe me. I found something. I knew when to go, I knew when to leave, I knew when to come back. I found something, always did. Still do." Crooking his thumb into his chest with each "I."

"I bet you do Joe," I responded, laughing.

I wasn't just humoring him. The more Joe's story unraveled, the more pronounced the layers of his intuition became. I had to keep reminding myself that he was fifteen (fifteen!) when he made this series of right choices between life and death. He was generally nonchalant about all of this. In this one instance, though, he seemed to recognize his ingenuity and take pride in it. I loved that he did. Loved his bravado and street smarts and how honestly and naturally he came upon them (even as I hated the world that created the need for these things). Loved that, in the midst of all of this evidence of the putrid depths humanity can sink to, here was a man who told his would-be tormentors where to stick it.

***

I get why Joe's family was so anxious about the Joe Boxer section. Part of me feels guilty for insisting on keeping it the way it is, curses a-plenty. The rest of me feels guilty for not showing more compassion that day at the Corner Bakery, for jumping so quickly into a space of antagonism, for dragging Joe into that space with me. I mean, *I get it*. Joe's family wants to protect and preserve Joe's memory. Of course they do, and I should have acknowledged this openly. This is a burden that all families of all survivors must share: these stories, these testimonies, are living monuments. These are stories that must be told, again and again, like the curse of the Ancient Mariner,[20] so that they're not forgotten. I get it that, for Joe's family (and perhaps for many families of many Holocaust survivors), there's something about Joe's cursing, about his getting angry, that compromises his function as a human monument.

It's just that Joe was so *happy*, so alive when he told this story. As deftly as he rushed through his descriptions of Dachau, wanting to distance himself from memories of his emaciation, he lingered here, luxuriating in these details. To me, it speaks volumes about Joe's sense of himself that he loves telling *this* story, in *this* way. I didn't want to take that away from him.

It reminded me of a story my dad liked to tell. He told it affectionately, lovingly, wistfully.

"So, it's August, 1980. The Eagles are headed into their fourth season with Vermeil. They'd made it to the playoffs the last two years, so they raked you over the coals with the goddamned tickets. I was in-between jobs, and, well, didn't have much in the way of extra cash. But, damn, the season was shaping up to be a good one. I had to find a way to get there. Jaworski, my God, the guy's a friggin' monster.

"So, it seems I'm going be sitting this one out—stuck watching the games on the tube at Ground Round. Can't believe my shitty luck, to be out of a job the year the Eagles are taking home division champs. I'd always been right there with them, job or no job, watching them slog it through. Of course, they sucked so bad the tickets were cheaper then.

"Pretty bleak overall. But then, Sherry. Oh, Sherry. Crazy, loud, red-headed Sherry. She takes me out to Frank's Deli for lunch one day, says she wants to go at an off-time, 2:00 or something, so it will be less crowded and we can be alone together. I'm fine with that: this woman's a fox.

"So, we're done eating and go out to the parking lot. Just as we get out there, this black stretch limo comes around the corner, drives into the lot, and comes to a stop right in front of us. The windows are completely dark—tinted, you know—I can't see anything through them. I have no idea what's going on, but I'm kind of nervous. I told you, this chick is crazy, I never knew what she was going to do from one minute to the next. So, the car rolls up to us, and the back window on the passenger side comes down about an inch, inch and a half. And out of the window comes two fingers holding an envelope. I look at Sherry, she grins, and says, 'take it, dummy.' So I do.

"The car squeals off and it's just me and her there in the parking lot again. 'Open it,' she says. I do. Inside are season-friggin'-tickets, box seats at Veteran's Stadium.

"Turns out, her dad's with the mob. The *Jewish* mob. I didn't even know there *was* a Jewish mob. I'm not going to mess with them, but, damn, I've gotta say I'm pretty impressed. Season-friggin' tickets in a playoffs year."

When I remember my dad's face as he told this story, the incredulous admiration that he expresses for these Jews who do whatever it takes to get exactly what they want—what *he* wants—something clicks. The story is an admission on my dad's part: Jews are expected to act in a certain, law-abiding way, to follow the rules. He admits here that he doesn't expect such brazen behavior, such transparent, bad-boy antics from Jews, certainly not in the world of football.

I think it's fair to say that, in this moment, my dad experienced his Jewishness in a new way, or that he saw the possibility for a different kind of Jewishness. Until I heard his story, I didn't know there was such a thing as the Jewish mob. All of a sudden, the Jewish man became a MAN, a dangerous and wholly more attractive possibility than the caricature I carried around in my head. And all of a sudden, I had a category into which I could place my dad that would account for the fact that he never *seemed* Jewish to me. Because, as aggressively as that stretch limo defied his expectations, he defied mine.

I hadn't thought about this story or my dad's telling it for years. The memory came back when, in preparing to write Joe's story, I read Rich Cohen's *Tough Jews*[21] (an account of the Jewish-American mob) and *The Avengers*[22] (an account of Jewish resistance fighters during and after the Holocaust). Cohen suggests that the mob and the Jewish resistance represent two forms of Jewishness that disrupt the stereotypes that we—as readers, viewers, listeners—bring to the table. The disruption is almost entirely oppositional: where we expect passivity, they give us aggression; where we expect cerebral, they give us muscle, body, blood; where we expect docile victim, they give us avenging victor. Swagger, swagger, swagger, as far as the eye can see.

We don't expect a Jewish mob, and we don't expect Holocaust survivors to so deftly master—on their own terms—the system calculated to destroy them. We seem to clamor for martyrs and redeemers. For clean and clear moral guidelines.

TOO-DELIBERATE STITCHES

I'm sitting on the train headed for my second Wacker Drive board-room visit with Joe. Stopped, once again, on the tracks to yield to a freight car. I'd brought with me my marked up copy of Sylvia Plath's collection, *Ariel*, somehow thinking that confronting this particular literary demon would help me gather my thoughts for the meeting. Now, I pulled it out of my bag, sensing that my annoyance with the stalled train was a fitting headspace to be in for this confrontation.

Sylvia's poem "Daddy"[23] has always angered me, from the self-absorbed and endless tirade against her tyrannical "Nazi" father, to her pretentious Boston-Brahmin delivery of the thing (which, for teaching purposes, I've forced myself to endure on more than one occasion). She's three stanzas into it when she begins weaving her own memory of her father (who died, if we can take the poem's word for it, when she was ten) with a generic account of the Holocaust. And then she waltzes in to take center stage in a drama that she constructs, in a "memory" that she has no business claiming as her own.

In the marginal notes that bleed furiously all over my copy of the poem, I can chronicle my own visceral response. Things start to get particularly thorny for me in this stanza:

An engine, an engine
Chuffing me off like a Jew.
A Jew to Dachau, Auschwitz, Belsen.
I began to talk like a Jew.
I think I may well be a Jew.

Next to the stanza, in pencil markings that grow steadily darker the more indignant I become, I've written: "What does it mean to take on this history if it's <u>not</u> your own? Is there an ethical problem with this equating of <u>all</u> victims? Is genocide the same as a suppressive child-hood or womanhood? No!"

Leaving aside the embarrassment I feel in re-reading the "teach-ing" questions I've prepared here (a total violation of Cardinal Teaching Rule #1: questions are supposed to be open-ended, not explicitly answered, lest they shut down discussion before it has begun), I find this outburst telling. It reveals to me something about my own assumptions and expectations concerning *who* can and cannot speak about the Holocaust, and *how* someone should speak, if I've deemed she has the right to do so. It's all there in black and white, in my knee-jerk and provincial and self-righteous response: this is not *her* history, this is not *her* story to tell. She has no connection to this history and she's morally suspect in attempting to establish a connection. How dare she speak of her own personal problems in the same breath as Auschwitz? She's a blond-haired, blue-eyed *shickse*, for God's sake!

I'm not proud of this response. Not at all. In addition to my irrational conviction that this poem would somehow be more appealing, more appropriate, if Sylvia happened to be Jewish, there is, as you can see, a fair amount of the whole "pot calling the kettle" business going on here. I recognize that much of my annoyance is probably fueled by a petty jealousy that, before I could articulate the intimate connection between my relationship with my own "daddy" and my obsession with the Holocaust, she'd already captured in vivid color the seductive quality of those grainy images we carry around, collectively, in black and white:

Not God but a swastika
So black no sky could squeak through.
Every woman adores a Fascist,
The boot in the face, the brute
Brute heart of a brute like you.

I'm bowled over by the power of this stanza.

And yet, and yet, I can't seem to help it. I haven't read or taught this poem for years—having dutifully excised it from my syllabus once I recognized how deep my animosity ran and, therefore, how ill-equipped I am to teach it. But as I read it again now on this train, I still find the poem, and the first stanza in particular, so thoroughly insensitive. So inexpressibly violent. I cringe with the brutality of her repetitive use of the word "Jew" like a finger jabbing me in the chest, shoving me away, naming me as other. Can't she hear the repeated offense in this term, the English equivalent of the derogatory term Yid? Doesn't she *know*, doesn't she *care* that someone like Joe—someone for whom this term represented a direct path to the loss of his *entire* family—might feel assaulted by these lines?

I am angry with Sylvia for her narcissism, her lack of empathy, her lack of concern for how deeply words can injure.

"Have you ever been to see the camps? Any of them?" Joe asked me during our last visit.

We had just eaten lunch. Napkins and sandwich crusts had been pushed to the edges of the table so we could get back to business.

I described for him my failed trip to Buchenwald. I was twenty-one, backpacking alone through Europe. I had planned to go, but landed there on a Monday, the day when most businesses and tourist sites (concentration camps apparently among them) are closed in Germany. I confessed to Joe my relief at the information, and told him that, instead, I accepted the invitation of a theology student from Jena to spend the afternoon and evening with her and some of her friends. The next morning, I looked out the window as the train crept past the station at Buchenwald and continued back on to Weimar. It did not occur to me to get off.

"I'll tell you what I think," Joe said to me. "I think you were afraid. You were afraid to go into the camp because you were afraid that you wouldn't be able to live with what you saw there."

Freud says there are no accidents. I think I knew the Monday-policy. I could have checked the hours and days of operation more diligently. I didn't. And my clear desire not to go was compounded by my decision to ride back through the station in question, now on a day when the camp was open, watching as it receded into the distance. In my defense, I *did* force myself to look at the guard-tower that I could see (or imagined I could see) from my seat by the train window. And that one image that I saw (or imagined I saw) has haunted me as the symbol of all that I couldn't or wouldn't look squarely in the face.

"Well, that's what it was," Joe concluded. "There was something in your body, in your heart, in your mind that told you not to go. Something told you *go* and *don't go*. You say you were happy that it was closed. And since it was closed you figured it was off your heart. Am I right or wrong?"

"Yes, I was relieved when I found out it was closed," I admitted.

"Okay. So that's it. You were afraid. You were afraid of what you would see and you didn't want to see what happened there."

"I guess I don't know what my seeing it does. What would it mean for me to see it? I mean, I feel, every day, I feel horrible about it—I don't know what—"

He cut me off.

"Something in your body, in your heart, in your mind told you not to go. Why, I don't know. Because you might be afraid to see it, because you might have to live with it, because it's going to be always on your mind. Many, many things. Many. Not one. Which, being Jewish, you probably would have gone if you had some other Jewish people with you, if you had a group."

"I wouldn't," I told him. "I'm not part of groups... I don't go in groups."

"You go by yourself," Joe said, giving me the benefit of the doubt.

"Yeah, just, I don't know." I knew I sounded defensive. I felt defensive.

"I just want to find out why you didn't. There must have been *something* there." Joe's jaw was set tightly, his right eyebrow raised, part skepticism, part bewilderment. All detective.

"Yeah, I don't know," I told him. "I did start out planning to go, and then when it was the wrong day, I didn't try to go again the next day. I mean, I did the same thing when I went to a seminar in Washington at the Holocaust Center. There are seminar rooms up on the third floor, and I was there for two weeks and didn't go through the museum, because I found it very... troubling... the way they make you go through it. Have you been to that museum?"

Joe didn't answer. His eyebrow arched higher.

"I mean, you get a card, and they take you through this whole sort of process and at the end you find out if you lived or you died, and I was sickened by the idea that the only experience someone would have would be either to be relieved that they lived or personally saddened that they died, and I had a real problem with that, too. And I don't think it's because I don't want to see or confront it, but it's just that... I don't know... this, here, what we're doing, feels to me like confronting it, and it's confronting it in a way that I don't know the camps would."

Still no response from Joe.

I gave up. Picked at my fingernails, refusing to look at him.

"I don't know, maybe I'm just being a coward."

"You were being something."

We both laughed then. He'd called bullshit.

"So, let me ask you something else," Joe said, loosening his jaw, ready to try again. "You were a kid then, when you went before. You went to Germany with your rucksack like the kids do and you didn't know nothing. But now, you're a woman, 37 years old, married, with children. You know more about life. You know more about what happened there. If I would say to you right now, 'Beth, let's go to Germany. I'll take you to see the camps,' would you do it? Would you go right now?"

"I would do it for you," I told him honestly, no hesitation.

"No, no. Not for me."

"No, that's why I would do it. I would go so I could understand your experience better."

"Would you go with me?" Joe circled back.

"I would, if I could just drop everything, I would."

"I'm not telling you to go by yourself." His voice was firm; we were in negotiations.

"No, I would, with you. Because that would be different, because we have a relationship, because I know you and I know what you went through."

"So, with me you would go."

"With you."

"But not on your own?"

"I... I don't think so."

"That's fine. That's fine. I just want to see the in and out. You would go with me because we have a certain relationship. Then you would go. Which... I can see that. No, no, I can see that because it's me, so you wouldn't be afraid. But by yourself you wouldn't go, not even today?"

"Well, I mean, there's more of a chance that I'd go now."

"But if you could go with me, you would?"

"Well, yes, because then it's connected to you, and it would help me to know you better and that's very important to me."

"Well, we can see there's different things in life. With me you would go, somebody else, no." Joe brushed his hands together, signaling that we had an understanding.

"I guess what I'm wondering is… from your end… do you think I need to go?"

I knew what the answer would be.

"I would definitely like to see you go. It's *your people* who went through it. I know what you're saying and I know how you feel. You were 21 years old then, you didn't know nothing about nothing, you were a little girl. But I'm talking about NOW. Now you've got everything open for you, and you know, and you read, you see this and that, so you probably would."

Something in me just couldn't let him think that.

"I still don't know if I would, because I don't know what to do with that. So I see it? Then what?"

"You're afraid that what you see… that you'll see it's not right," he said calmly, slowly, definitively.

I responded, less so, "I *know* it's not right… it's horrific, what happened… but there's nothing in my seeing it that would make it anything other than it was."

"Well, definitely. It's terrible the way it is."

I continued, undeterred, "And I *do* feel like, for a very long time, I've been confronting this every day. And it's one of the things I think about: why do people go? What is it they're trying to get there? What is it they achieve?"

He looked hard at me. Shook his head. Said quietly, "People lost family. People lost mothers, fathers, children."

But still I couldn't just give up and give in.

"I *know*. But other people who didn't lose anybody. Who go because it's something that they think they're supposed to do. And then they go and have lunch somewhere afterwards."

I nearly spat this last sentence out. We'd laid bare the core of it for me.

"No, no. *Not them*," Joe was starting to raise his voice. "Other people have no interest because it didn't hit them. They didn't suffer from it. So we can forget about them. But I'm talking about *our* people. You. I. My kids. Your parents. Whatever. *Jewish* people… I mean, there's not a Jew living who didn't go to the Holocaust museum to see… not a Jewish person or Jewish child... now, not only Jewish kids. Gentiles, they bring in everybody. In Illinois, you know, they teach it in the schools, and the kids come in buses to the museum in Skokie, you'd be surprised how many non-Jewish people come to the museum."

It seemed to me we were talking past one another.

"People have to know the history, they have to know what happened. But what I don't understand is this: why do you have to go to the places where so many people died? Why can't you go to the places where they lived?"

"It's got nothing to do with it. People know about it. People do know about it. Jewish and not Jewish. But Jewish people, they want to see, they want to know. They know what happened. They go because their parents... they lost the whole *mishpuchah*... they lost everybody. They're by themselves. That's why they go. You know how many people were here when they opened up the memorial in Skokie? 2,600. *Two thousand.* All Jews. Basically all Jews. Why do you think 2,600 people go to see it?" More than vaguely indignant at this point.

"They have to go," I conceded. "They have to see it. But don't you think that's different from going to Buchenwald?"

"Well, not necessarily. You go to Buchenwald today, they've got cards... 'this is this, this is that'... they show you everything. But the fact is that you don't have to go there. I'm not saying that you have to go there. But every Jewish person should go and does go."

That stung. Especially following so closely on the coattails of his earlier declaration that "there's not a Jew living who didn't go to the Holocaust museum." Those two statements announced to me Joe's opinion of what makes a good Jew. I had failed in this regard, twice, in quick succession.

Joe told me then about his daughter, who had wanted to see everything. How he went to Poland with her, sixty-two years after the war and his vow to never, ever return. "There's nothing good I can say about Poland," he told me, "nothing at all." But he went with her to every camp in which he had been imprisoned, and then some. He went with her, because she wanted and needed to see those places that had not claimed her father.

"And so you see," he continued, "there's you and there's her. She wanted to know, to see. You, you are not, I wouldn't say interested, but something inside you says you can't go because, after seeing it, you wouldn't be able to sleep at night."

"I already can't sleep at night," I informed him. "Does it upset you that I haven't gone?"

"What?" Joe was genuinely taken aback.

"Does it upset you?"

"No, no, no. Now you are going through it with me and with this."

"Well, the thing is, I've gone through it. Everything I've ever worked on is about the Holocaust. It's very personal now, because now your face is connected to it."

"Yeah," Joe said, "Otherwise, you wouldn't. You wouldn't know nothing about the Holocaust."

"*Nooo,*" I said, much more forcefully than I expected to. "I'm telling you, everything I've ever done has been about the Holocaust. Everything. Everything I've ever done has been about the Holocaust. And you are..."

"I am it."

"*Nooo,*" I said again, impatiently. "I've written books before this. I've written articles."

"Oh, okay," Joe responded, taking it all with a grain of salt, mercifully. "But now you do more?"

"This is just another stage." Unbearably cold. And not true. "Everything I've ever worked on has been about the Holocaust, everything I've ever written. Everything. This is my life. This has been my life, and it's why I'm so interested in you, because now it's personal... it's connected to you."

"Because I'm the living part of this."

"Yes, *you're* the living part of this. But I haven't been avoiding this," I repeated, needing him to understand.

"This is hell. Today, in our times, hell must be like this."

Primo Levi wrote this, describing the Holocaust universe in general, but in particular a moment of ruthless sadism upon his arrival at Auschwitz. After four days without water, he and a truckload of men were deposited in a room with a tap with a sign reading *Wassertrinken verboten* (drinking the water is forbidden) over it. "Hell must be like this," Levi insists, "we are tired, standing on our feet, with a tap which drips while we can't drink the water, and we wait for something which will certainly be terrible, and nothing happens and nothing continues to happen. What can one think about? One cannot think any more, it is like being already dead."[24]

Again on the train, headed back home after an exhausting day, thinking about Levi and trying to process the many glimpses of hell that Joe and I had talked about. Among them:

The fatal truck ride with his father:

People pushed more persistently, more defiantly. Joe and his father were jostled and pressed against the tailgate of the truck. It suddenly fell open. No time for discussion, they took the only chance they both sensed they had.

Joe's father jumped. Joe followed instantly. Other men jumped, some fell out behind them.

Not missing a beat, the police open fired, spraying bullets everywhere. They shot at everyone—at the people running frantically on the ground and at those who remained huddled on the truck.

The noise was deafening: Germans shouting, Jews screaming, shots tearing through flesh and sky. Bodies fell to the ground in crashing waves.

The cattle car ride from Rakow to Buchenwald:

The guards divided them into two groups, leading each to a separate set of cattle cars. Joe walked with the others onto a closed car, people crowding around him, pressing against him, squeezing into a space that had been filled to capacity ten times over. No room to sit down, no seats even if there had been. The doors shut behind them, locks clicking into position without remorse. It went dark inside the car, save for a sliver of light delivered through the barbed wire of the tiny window on the top corner of the car. The same window offered a breath of air, stingily parceled out among them. The whole car was filled with noxious sweat and the unmistakable stench of human waste. Bodies responding unwillingly and reflexively to conditions designed to produce exactly these results. This, Joe realized, was what people must have meant when they said they could smell fear.

The death march:
They marched out of the camp in one long column, ten prisoners across and several hundred deep, German officers flanking them. In the freezing cold, nothing to wrap around them for warmth, heavy shoes with soles made of wood or no soles at all, they marched through the day and into the night and back again.

People fell to the ground in exhaustion, unable to go any farther. They were shot on the spot. Bodies piled up on each side of the road as the column moved on at a steady pace. Impossible to stop and help; a gesture of empathy answered by a bullet to the head.

I pulled out the draft I'd been working on and read these passages again slowly, more conscious than ever of the chasm between Joe's horrifying lived reality and my limited capacity to *truly* imagine this reality. I heard again Levi's admission of his "violent, immediate need" to show this hell to "the rest." And Joe's explanation for why people go to the camps: "they go because their parents... they lost the whole *mishpuchah*... they lost everybody. They're by themselves." And realized this: in both Levi's and Joe's statements, there is profound isolation, two people standing alone across a divide—one carrying the weight of a story that must be communicated, the other, devastated by a story that she herself did not live.

The handful of Jewish students at DePauw who identify strongly enough with their Judaism to have joined Hillel are responsible for bringing a speaker to campus for Yom HaShoah (Holocaust Remembrance Day). Most of the time, they select someone from the directory of survivors in the region provided by the Jewish Federation of Greater Indianapolis. They take this responsibility seriously, passing it on each year to the next class as the seminal charge of the organization, the charge to preserve the memory of the Holocaust. Their modest budget goes almost exclusively to funding this event. Traditionally, the talk is given in East College, the oldest building on campus, which used to serve as chapel in the days when DePauw was officially tied to the Methodist Church. Campus lore holds that the building is haunted by the ghosts of lovelorn and anxious students, who either plunged or clumsily fell to their deaths from the bell-tower. Now the former chapel, with its rows of pews, pipe-organ, high-vaulted ceiling and stained-glass windows, is used as a venue for honored guests. Most of the time, the speaker draws a decent crowd.

I thought about this en route to Joe, the train lurching unexpectedly, jostling me to wonder why this year the room had been as close to empty as I'd ever seen it. People had scattered in clumps of three or four on the pews, some sitting in the back rows, a sea of emptiness between them and the speaker on stage—Meyer Bronicki, a member of the Bielski Brothers, a partisan group that rescued Jews and fought against the Nazis in German-occupied Poland. The sparseness of the crowd had been surprising; the Bielski Brothers were the subject of the Oscar-nominated film, *Defiance*, which had arrived in theatres several months before. The student in charge of organizing Meyer's visit introduced him, provided the details of his story, then remained on stage with him to help guide him from point to point in his recounting of his story and to field questions. I fought with myself for judging the length of her skirt (too short) and the height of her heels (too high).

I looked around, trying to read people's faces. For a while, people listened soberly, nodding their heads, looking sad and sick, alternately drawn in by and distanced from the words spilling out of the small man sitting on stage in front of them. The late afternoon sunlight refracted through the stained glass, lulling us with kaleidoscopic patterns on the floor and pews. As Meyer's story went on, the thread became more difficult to follow, details compounding in their own contextual framework, intricate and inaccessible. I saw people stifling yawns, glancing surreptitiously at their watches, checking their phones.

As I processed it all on the train that morning, I realized that I had been wondering: what is the optimal length of time for this kind of event, a service of remembrance? What is our threshold for listening to—for hearing—the story of someone else's pain? When do we shut down, our day-to-day concerns and obligations asserting themselves over a past that can be mourned but never recovered? And what are we *doing*, when we listen to these accounts, if we can't possibly feel—inhabit—the pain someone else went through?

***

I don't agree with Joe that going to the places where people lived (as opposed to where they died) "has got nothing to do with it." I think, actually, that it's got everything to do with it—if "it" means coming face to face with the enormity of loss.

I went to Prague in 2002, one stop on a winter-term-abroad class on "Coffee House Culture" that I led with another faculty member. I managed to sneak away one day to commune with Kafka and to greet the city on my own terms. I wandered around the Kafka museum for a bit, disappointed by the way my hero had been wrapped up and cleanly packaged for tourists. I left quickly, preferring the misty January air to the too-glaring lights of the museum (and feeling pretty confident that Kafka would have preferred it, too). Wandering behind the museum, away from the Old Town Square, I turned onto a cramped street and found myself face to face with the Old-New Synagogue, Kafka's synagogue.

I hadn't realized it was so close.

Just beyond the Altneuschul, was the Jewish Museum, which actually consists of six synagogues converted into a memorial for the dead and a safeguard for the living. Most of the synagogues still conduct services, alongside of exhibits filled with artifacts of Jewish practice, ritual, and culture. That services continue in these glorious buildings is itself a gesture of the starkest defiance, a proverbial finger in the eye to the Nazi project that was responsible for amassing the museum's holdings and that lent support to its establishment (the idea was that this would serve as a keepsake of an extinct race).

One of these synagogues—the Pinkas Synagogue—is the permanent home of a collection of drawings by the children of Terezin. There, in that ghetto that served both as a way station (Jews were brought here with the express purpose of deporting them to killing centers and concentration camps) and as a massive propaganda site (the Nazis pitched it as a place where families could voluntarily admit their infirm or elderly members for rest as they waited out the war), imprisoned artists chose to give children art lessons. They encouraged the children to draw their daily experiences in the camp, to keep memory books,

112

where they might document their dreams and fears, their dwindling hope. Of the fifteen thousand children who passed through there, it is estimated that fewer than 100 survived.

Here's where I loitered, in this room, with these drawings. I don't remember if I passed the memorial to the nearly 80,000 murdered Czech Jews (also in this synagogue) before or after I found my way to this room. I don't remember if I was already numb when I walked in and saw the first drawing, or if it was seeing the first drawing that knocked the wind out of me. I don't remember the drawings themselves. All I remember is the way the room swayed and swelled, the collective, brightly-colored images blurring together, as the weight of it all hit me. I hadn't known it was coming, and, so, couldn't prepare myself for it: the horrible, awful, grotesque truth that the children who had created these pictures had been murdered. Without pity, without remorse, without justice.

In that conversation about the camps, Joe and I had wandered into a long-nursed psychic minefield, and old wounds are slow to close. We were skirting around that emotionally charged territory of Jewish identity politics, and I'd felt cornered, judged, found lacking. What kind of Jew doesn't go to the camps? What kind of Jew refuses to go through the United States Holocaust Memorial Museum?

I named the elephant in the room.

"I think I may not be the kind of Jew you think is a good Jew. I'm not *that* kind of Jew."

I laughed as I said this, but it was nervous laughter.

"No, no, no, no," Joe said, waving away my anxiety. "There's no such thing. A Jew is a Jew. Remember, you got your feelings. You do however you feel, and there's no reason for me to tell you you're not a good Jew. You have your feelings, and you should. You feel that way and that's okay. I'm not criticizing you for that. NO. Not at all. I just want to know how you feel about it. That's all. That's it. And, eh, that's the whole thing."

His repetition of and emphasis on the word NO convinced me. Joe wasn't holding this against me.

That bullet dodged, my resistance to going to see the camps still seems quasi-pathological, especially given that I *do* have a tendency to bring everything back to the Holocaust (even if my insistence that *everything* I've ever done has been about the Holocaust was certainly, well, overblown).

I've never really understood the *push to see*. The pressure exerted by institutional Judaism to bear witness to the Holocaust by visiting the camps has never made sense to me. What good does *this* kind of bearing witness do?

Before this talk with Joe, my reasoning had been clear. To look was to violate, to provide a concrete image of—and therefore limitations to—what has always seemed to me a necessarily unseeable (as opposed to unspeakable) set of horrors. I am the most secular of Jews, but, even so, something in my anxiety about seeing (and not-seeing) feels vaguely connected to the second commandment. The prohibition against graven images taps into a basic psychological truth: what we can see, we can know; conversely, we can never fully know what remains unseen. The prohibition forces us into the more difficult space of not-knowing, the unsettling position of never having closure.

It had seemed to me, before this talk, that it would be too *simple* to see: an easy way out. I'd look, I'd see, I'd be done with it. Case closed.

But the way Joe zeroed in on how I would go *with him*, how he dwelled on the difference between going with him and not going—that changes things. I *would* go with him. It's hard to describe the surge of adrenalin, the sense of possibility, when I hear Joe ask me, "If I were to say to you right now, Beth, let's go to the camps, would you do it?"

When I listen to this conversation on the recording, I hear how my defensiveness ramps up when Joe starts comparing me to his daughter. I hear it when he describes, at length, the trip he took with her. My defensiveness, laid bare, seems to be pretty much your garden-variety jealousy.

What I wouldn't give to have my dad back. What I wouldn't give to go on a trip with him, any trip, anywhere, even a trip to the camps.

But what *really* blindsided me was the twinge of sibling rivalry I felt—for someone who wasn't my sibling and with whom I had no need for rivalry.

***

There's a play by Samuel Beckett called "Krapp's Last Tape." It's about as low-budget a production as you could hope to find: one guy, sitting on stage with a reel-to-reel player. The action consists of him listening to recordings of several younger selves collecting their memories; the older recorded selves intrude with commentary on these memories, and the present-day self (the guy sitting all by himself on stage) plays the tapes, bit by bit, adding his own commentary to the mix. The result is a hall of mirrors, a hall of memories, bouncing and refracting off of one another as each remnant of self is both surpassed and captured for eternity.

Action-deficient though the play may be, it is thrilling. The way the memories accumulate and deepen, the way Krapp's *hearing* of the memories takes on new contours and emphases with each hearing. The way he moves from judging himself through these memories, from condemning himself and the choices he made, to acknowledging that these choices made him who he was in that moment he recorded. The way he comes to understand that these moments collectively add up to the man sitting on stage, and that that self, too, is temporary.

My relationship with Joe and with the telling of his story is as much or more about listening to our recorded conversations again and again as it is about anything else. I feel like Krapp as I listen to these recordings. As I listen, I hear our earlier conversations through the lens of later ones, I hear pauses in his descriptions of things, catches in my voice, chuckles, sighs and deep breaths that may mean nothing or everything, and may be overlooked, overemphasized or shaded differently depending on the hour or day or length of time I've been listening. These recordings are living documents, as alive or more to me now as they were the day they were recorded. And they're precious to me: they give me the chance to spend more time with Joe, to hear his voice, to be reminded that the act of storytelling—the act of telling *his* story—is something like that infinite loop that Krapp steps into.

***

This time, when I sit on that tattered couch listening to that conversation about the camps, I notice a few things. First, it was *long*: 36 minutes. And those 36 minutes sound totally different from any of the conversations that had come before. They are raw and vulnerable. We're almost having an argument. Before this conversation, things were pretty one-sided: I asked Joe questions, he gave me answers, even if they sometimes didn't answer the question I had just asked. Here, Joe turns the tables. He assumes the role of psychoanalyst. As much he resists my incessant Freudian mode, he puts me on the couch, refusing to let me get away with my hedging, refusing to let me lie to myself. He's looking for subtext, for deeper motivations.

The first time I processed this conversation, I heard Joe's statement—"I think you're afraid"—as an accusation, equating fear with weakness, judging me for my decision to bypass Buchenwald. This time around, my attention catches on the repetitive strain of these sorts of statements:

- "There must have been something that made you not want to go…"
- "Something in your body, in your mind, in your heart told you not to go. Why I don't know… Many, many things, not one…"

- "That's fine, that's fine. I just want to see the in and out of it…"
- "I just want to know how you FEEL about it. That's all. That's it. And that's the whole thing."

This time around, I hear—I *grasp*—how hard Joe was working to understand me, how he was struggling to make sense of my shortsighted thinking. For him, it's about the complexity, about uncovering the many possible reasons—emotional, physical, mental—I might have for not going. And I see that, in fact, there is no lasting judgment.

Rather than be insulted by my appalling arrogance—"I've written books… articles… I know everything"—he says, simply: "I just want to understand what you're feeling. That's it. That's all."

That's all? That's *everything*. That's unconditional recognition.

What I hear now is what I've always known. Joe *is* it: the only possible point of entry into the unfathomable horror that is the Holocaust. Without Joe, I could have read a million books, written a million more, and still not really known anything. Because it's not about *knowing*. And, despite the fact that I'm sure now that Joe is right, that I haven't gone to the camps because I am afraid, because I can't bear the thought of seeing these monuments of brutality and suffering, it's not about *seeing* either. It's about hearing. About trying to hear. About listening.

I start to understand the immediacy of recognition that visiting the camps can provide for people on both sides of the divide: the one with the story that needs to be told and the other, who's trying to process the magnitude of that story.

WEARING OUT A METAPHOR

There was one time when Joe didn't want me to look, didn't want me to *see*.

We were making our way through Question #5 on the list:

> ...the scene in the courtyard just before the truck ride to the cemetery. how many people were out there? what did the man who sold you out look like? what did his voice sound like when he told you he knew the apartment was yours and that you needed to step forward? what were you thinking about this guy? did your father say anything at any point?

Joe was explaining to me that, if he had had his way, he and his father never would have been out there in the courtyard. But his father was afraid, and, so, they gave into the orders of the Jewish police.

"Those sons of bitches," Joe said, banging his fist on the table, "they thought they were going to live, but they killed them too. The Jewish kapo, he said to my father, 'You better come out. I have to tell them that you're living in the building.' But I gave him a dirty look. I knew that those people are no fucking good. I told my father, and I was right."

Computer in front of me, I busily recorded his words in an attempt to steel myself against the part that I knew was coming next. Trying to be businesslike, to get the facts down. I cleared my throat a little, took a breath that felt deeper than usual and asked:

"And the truck ride was rather short, right? The ride to the cemetery. They planned to get you all the way to the cemetery, but the problem was people got... it happened on the street... on the way." *It.* Impersonal pronoun.

"That's right," Joe said.

"Did you, um, in the truck, were you talking with your father at all? I mean, were you able to have any kind of conversation with him? I know it must have been crazy..."

"We knew already where we were going." His voice was quiet, resigned.

119

"You did know, because the Poles are out there yelling at you," me, putting the pieces together of the story I'd read before in draft form.

"They knew where the cemetery is. I never had been to the cemetery, but the people on the truck, they knew. They were crying, and crying. So, the Polacks, they're standing on the side of the street. They knew where we were going, And they told us, *Zyd*, you know *Zyd*, it's *Jude*. And they're saying, you know what they did? 'Give us your money.' Lousy Polacks. Real lousy."

"But you... I'm trying to imagine what it must have been like for you... I mean... on that truck... you knew... you knew where you were going, your father knew. Did you hold each other?"

Joe's voice was still quiet. "No, we didn't hold each other, because the end of the truck, see, this is the end of the truck here. My father and I were staying over here, and there were so many people we could hardly stand, and all of a sudden, the door... here... it burst... and the back opened up, you see, it opened up. And when it did, I jumped, and my father jumped, and so many other people did. And the police, they're right here behind us... they started shooting at us. You see, this is us in the truck with the open back, this is the other people, this is the police car, they're shooting at us over here. So, I don't know how I did it. So I dropped on the pavement and I played dead. Ok? So they didn't bother me. They shoot all the other ones, the ones who were on the floor already, they shoot. And then, the rest of the ones who did not jump, they had to take them back to the cemetery. So, after they left, I got up. I went to that house, you know, where the Polacks live, and you know the rest."

As he did the day he described the battle in the War of Independence, Joe was sketching things out here on a piece of paper to show me what was happening. His sketching momentarily diverted me from the nausea that was building.

"So, in the truck ride... how long were you in the truck before this all happened? Five minutes? Ten minutes?"

"A few minutes."

"And, in those minutes, if you can, like, block out everything else that was happening... just you and your father... can you... can you think of what..."

And then I started to cry. I had tried hard not to, but it was too much to think about Joe experiencing these minutes and their aftermath. So much terror, so much cruelty, so much loss. So little I could do to fix any of these things. So much I wanted to fix.

Men in their early-to-mid-twenties, in Dockers and collared shirts with smart but understated prints, walked by the boardroom. They glanced over at us through the glass, barely curious.

"Come over here," Joe said to me, ignoring them. "Come over here. Stop it. Stop it."

I put the computer on the table and rolled my chair close to Joe, facing him, my face covered in tears. He took both my hands and held them in his.

"Don't worry, don't worry. I know how you feel."

How I felt was ridiculous, weak, despicable. *Him* comforting *me*? After all he'd been through, and I couldn't even muster up the strength to listen to his story without breaking down?

"I'm so sorry," I said to him, embarrassed, still gulping back sobs and making squeaking noises. "I can't even imagine what that would be like."

Joe patted me on the back, hard, as if trying to physically push the image away.

"Don't," he said, definitively. "Don't try. Don't even try. Don't try to imagine it. Okay? Don't cry. Please. I did it already for you once, right?"

We both laughed, remembering that first meeting at his daughter's house.

"I know. I know. I'm sorry. I'm terrible. This is awful."

Joe pulled my head towards him and planted a noisy, wet kiss there.

"I know, baby. I know. It's okay." Joe said, in that rhythmic voice we use to soothe our children.

"Okay, but I really, I do need to know what happened then," I told him, trying to gather any remaining scrap of professionalism. Hard to pull off, as I was still wiping my nose on a napkin. "Because people are going to want to know. Were you talking to him? Praying?"

He laughed, drily. But he was serious again as he said, "Don't. That's okay. That's okay, dear. Don't worry about it. That's it. It's something that you have to, need to… I don't mean to make you do something like this, but that's the way it was."

"No, it's the way it has to be. It's absolutely the way it has to be."

"Right. There's nothing you can do."

He looked at me, kissed the top of my head again.

"*Shana madela (beautiful girl)*," he said, and laughed again.

***

I sat on the train back to Indiana thinking about the weight of that conversation and what it meant that Joe seemed to want to push the image of his father dying out of my head. Why push it out, when all he wanted was for people to *see*, to *know* what he went through? And I couldn't stop thinking about why, after so much conversation about looking and not-looking, I was still having trouble letting go of the feeling I had had when I attended the seminar at the United States Holocaust Memorial Museum in Washington.

Here's how the website describes the permanent exhibit that I couldn't bring myself to walk through:

> Visitors to the United States Holocaust Memorial Museum's Permanent Exhibition receive ID cards chronicling the experiences of people who lived in Europe during the Holocaust. These cards are designed to help personalize the historical events of the time.
>
> Each identification card has four sections: The first provides a biographical sketch of the person. The second describes the individual's experiences from 1933 to 1939, while the third describes events during the war years. The final section describes the fate of the individual and explains the circumstances—to the extent that they are known—in which the individual either died or survived.

I understand what the identification cards are for. Personalizing the history makes it real for people. But, that last part, that "describes the fate in which the individual either died or survived" part, still strikes me as the most grotesque of strategies. The motives still seem aimed at the very worst of human nature. *This* is what I was trying—inelegantly—to express to Joe. What am I supposed to do—how am I supposed to feel—when I learn "my" fate?

It seems like I've got two options:

123

a) I can feel lucky, chosen maybe, somehow personally responsible for escaping death.

or

b) I can feel paralyzed with fear, sickened, nauseous at the thought of the death "I" could not escape.

But can I feel empathy? Can I make an actual connection with the person on the card?

Every time I think about it, I can't help but imagine the busloads of teenagers arriving *en masse* at the museum, forced at this precise developmental moment of constitutional thoughtlessness to witness something that can't help but trigger an opportunity for competition and/or cruelty. "Ha, ha," one would say to another, elbowing him in the ribs, "you're dead. See ya later, sucker." And it wouldn't be their fault that they'd have no way to process this information. How could they?

***

On June 10, 2009, as I was compiling the first draft of The Suit, a man walked into the Holocaust Museum in Washington with a gun and opened fire, killing a security guard. Other guards fired back, critically injuring him. The man was 88 years old, a long-time white supremacist and Holocaust denier.

The scene played itself over and over in my mind throughout the day, each time picking up new details that I would obsess about. I thought about the 39-year-old security guard, about the panic and horror he must have felt in those last moments, the powerlessness, the rage, the desperation when he came face-to-face with the knowledge that his life was over. I thought about the people in the lobby, scattering in terror when they became aware of an armed gunman in their midst. Did they call their loved ones, thinking that they were going to die, here, now, in this building? Did they crouch down on the floor, shielding their heads and those of their children, praying silently or fervently that they would be spared?

My husband tells me how unhealthy and morbid it is to do this kind of visualization. I know he's right, but I can't seem to help it. These sorts of things completely unhinge me: Shady Hook (dear God, Shady Hook), Columbine, September 11th, basically any incidence of people being trapped and at the mercy of others bent on destruction. I can't stop thinking about how these people, unlucky enough to be in the wrong place at the wrong time, come to terms with their impending deaths. About the thoughts that consume them. About the naked and fatal arbitrariness of it all.

This is morbid, yes, without a doubt. But it does seem to place into relief the question of why, as a general rule, these sorts of events occupy so much time and attention in the media. Why are these stories so compelling for so many of us? Why can't—why *don't*—we look away? This, too, is about *looking*, about the need to see the graphic scene play out before us, dramatization upon dramatization. Why does traffic slow to a crawl even *after* the accident debris has been cleared off the road? Why can't we help but crane our necks to see the shards of glass ourselves, the gore, the grisly aftermath? In those moments when I catch myself looking, I detect relief, which I push away in horror—*I'm still alive, my children are still alive*, we have managed to skirt this particular tragedy. A silent prayer takes over—*kain a hora, kain a hora*, keep the evil eye away, don't call attention to our escape, please oh please oh please.

Survivor's guilt: penance for *Schadenfreude*, unwitting, un-indulged, or not.

So what draws us to Joe's story, and to stories like his?

Is it that he lived to tell the tale? That he found himself, profoundly, in the wrong place at the wrong time, but was able to escape the trap set for him? We call Joe and others "survivors." As much as it attempts to describe these people in their own context, the term might say more about the role that they play for us. We label them by the generic act of survival, not distinguishing among the many small moments and decisions that accumulate in what becomes this one defining trait. Their ability to stay alive assures us that, however remote the possibility of survival may be, however random, it is nevertheless one possible outcome in the confrontation with the equally strong drive to destroy pulling in the other direction. We *need* to know this remote possibility exists. We need to know that our lives are not as precarious as these events would suggest, that there is more standing between us and our mortality than a man with a gun and a vendetta.

There's a book that sits on my shelf in the company of so many others on post-Holocaust philosophy and theology: *Morality After Auschwitz: The Radical Challenge of the Nazi Ethic*, by Peter Haas. My copy was used when I bought it, coming apart from the binding, and covered with someone else's high-lightings and comments. It sits next to Hannah Arendt's study of Adolf Eichmann, *The Banality of Evil*, quietly undermining her premise that evil can be at once absolute and utterly mundane. Haas's thesis is simple:

> "Europeans committed what we judge to be heinous crimes under Nazi rule not because they were deficient in moral sensibility, and not because they were quintessentially evil and brutal people, but because they were in fact ethically sensitive. They were fully aware of what they were doing and displayed prin-

cipled acquiescence. The difference is that for them such deeds were simply no longer understood to be evil. Under the influence of what I shall be calling the Nazi ethic, vast numbers of people simply came to understand evil in different terms and, in perfectly predictable and comprehensible fashion, acted upon their understanding."[25]

It is nauseating to think of genocide as an "ethic," as part of an overarching system that made good, principled, sense to "ethically sensitive" people. But Haas' challenge is that we suspend judgment long enough to get inside the Nazi ideology. That we consider, first, that there is a consistent logic at work in this space and, second, that this logic compelled a whole society to redefine its values.[26] He's asking us to get inside the logic of the system, because the alternative—*not* doing this, casting this thinking off as "crazy" or "evil" or "other"—is supremely dangerous.

Haas is saying that I *have* to visualize, I have to try to understand what seems incomprehensible, even if it makes me nauseous. At the end of the day, there's some small—very small—comfort in Haas's thesis: humans tend to act, well, *ethically,* even if what that means changes from context to context.

My thoughts turn to the shooter. 88 years old. *Eighty-eight years old.* What kind of hatred is so strong that a person can carry it around for eighty-eight years?

I answer my own question in the tautological way that is second nature for most Jews, even the most divorced from the faith among us. Anti-Semitism, of course. The man is an anti-Semite, drenched in an irrational hatred for Jews, driven by his singular obsession that Jews are simultaneously subhuman and capable of demonic feats of power, like killing God and running Hollywood. And, coming to this conclusion that doesn't really answer anything about anything—least of all to shed light on this man's peculiar and idiosyncratic and probably internally consistent brand of irrationality—I began to feel very guilty for the kneejerk opinions I once held about the Holocaust Museum in Washington.

Because, it's starting to seem to me that maybe we need places like the Holocaust Museum precisely *because* there are people who would storm into them in a murderous rage, precisely *because* there are people who deny the event that they were built to memorialize. These places bear witness to truth. They defy resistance to that bearing witness. They grant our desire to see suffering. And they provide a framework to bestow that suffering with meaning.

***

For Joe, sickness equals dwelling, ruminating, getting stuck. And getting stuck, dwelling, is not conducive to survival.

What makes one person crack under pressures that aren't even really pressures—calling a stranger on the phone, for instance—while another person can go to hell and back, basically summing up the experience with a shrug of the shoulders and a "So it happened, life goes on" (Joe said exactly this on more than one occasion)? Is it purely circumstantial? Genetic? Constitutional?

Joe has varied theories on the subject. At times he is convinced that anyone in his situation would have done the same thing, at others he acknowledges that he might have had something to do with his survival. Somewhere between luck and savvy: the hazy space between playing out the hand you were dealt and throwing out the deck. Once, he showed me a newsletter from the Jews of Czestochowa Society, which provided a brief account of what happened there during the war.[27] There was also a commentary written by someone Joe knew, and Joe referred back to it several times, as if it captured more precisely his own thoughts about what it took to survive:

"The fact is, it tells you right here," he jabbed the piece of paper with his index finger, "that none of us were smarter than another, and it tells us right here that it was only luck. This guy did what he did in order to stay alive. I don't ask anybody how they did, because it's foolish. No one's going to come to me to tell me, 'how did you do it?' It worked for me, and that's all that counts. Somebody else does something else, do you see? And that's all that matters. You're alive. How do you stay alive? You know, you live the best you do, and I was lucky. You do what you can do. It's not that I was smart, or that someone told you what to do."

Primo Levi describes "the doctrine [he] was… to learn so hurriedly in the Lager" this way: "that man is bound to pursue his own ends by all possible means, while he who errs but once pays dearly."[28] It's a similar space of physical survival that Joe outlines. There's no path to follow, no blueprint, no precedent. You do what you have to do to survive, or you die. But to credit "smarts" with getting out alive is to give credit where it's not due. And it seems to be Joe's unspoken rule that

129

it is both distasteful and inappropriate to make distinctions and judgments concerning how people negotiated this space. *That* they survived is evidence enough, and the only valuable measure, of the effectiveness of their choices.

As for the *mental* space of survival that follows, the living-with-what-happened, Joe has no time for the haze of ambiguity. Here he makes a clear distinction between what works and what doesn't:

"Let me tell you something," he says. "Lots of Holocaust survivors, they were at different camps, whatever, they still, now, they dream, they feel, they still go around with an idea of what happened, and they need to go to shrinks. There are Holocaust people that still live from the Holocaust, they still live what they went through. And they're sick, because they're stuck in their minds. They do it to themselves. I wouldn't have it, I wouldn't do it. I never did. I never will," Joe literally beats his chest. "I take it as it was given to me and do what is right. You want to cry, cry to yourself, but don't cry to others, because everybody has their *pekl*."

Pekl means baggage, one's existential burden, as it were, a sack of rocks we all haul around with us. It's one of Joe's favorite Yiddish words, maybe because he's so used to carrying it without thinking twice about the fact that it's there.

There is more than a hint of judgment here, more than a mere suggestion that Joe finds the kind of hashing and re-hashing that therapy mandates a waste of time and energy.

Holocaust and post-Holocaust theology is a thriving academic field. At one point, I was in the thick of it and knew, firsthand, the seduction of puzzling through the intricacies of covenantal theology in the face of Auschwitz. Those books and articles I was so quick to let Joe know about, that day that we were quasi-arguing about my not-going to the camps—nearly all of them have something to do with all of this. I was so certain as I wrote them that I could figure it all out on paper, so sure that all I needed to do to gain an understanding of how faith could or could not exist in the midst of this horror was to parse each word of each poem, passage, line.

I sat on the train thinking about the hubris of this posture, about how irrelevant my cluttered theological and theoretical musings had been. And I realized that they no longer hold any attraction for me, because they have *nothing to do* with the way Joe processes his own experience, despite my attempts to try to get Joe to conform to and confirm the theories that once consumed me about how faith is challenged or disrupted or destroyed.

Turns out, all I needed to do was ask him what he believed, which I had done that day:

"I'm Conservative. Always have been—this hasn't changed at all." Joe responded matter-of-factly to the question I kept pestering him with.

"Really? Nothing's changed? You still believe everything you believed before the war?"

"You want me to say whether or not I have any problems with God, right? No, kid, I don't have any problems. Let him be him, let me be me. That's how I see it. How can you talk to somebody who doesn't answer? I leave him alone. I go to Temple on the Holidays and Shabbus. I go because I enjoy it, not because I'm trying to be a rabbi. I'm not a goy, okay? I'm a Jew. I like to go to Temple. My father went to Temple on the High Holidays. I go too. My kids are Reform. I have nothing against it, as long as they go. I would feel very bad if they didn't go, but they do. What's to God is to God, what's to you is to you, so everybody's happy."

Leave God alone? That had never occurred to me.

***

"Always go to the head, not to the feet," Joe was telling me. "That's how you have to do it, you hear me? Work your way up."

He was describing what it meant to make connections in Buchenwald. What it meant to survive. What it took to know and to play the game.

I jumped up unceremoniously, walked over to the window and looked out at Lake Michigan. We had been sitting for too long around that big table in that boardroom. I needed to stretch, to move, to get some circulation in my legs and brain. This slogging-through of Joe's memories was sometimes disorienting, the way it jutted up against the pace and stakes and frenetic energy of the memories themselves.

"I'm listening, Joe. I just need to stand for a while."

He gave me a thumbs-up.

"So, anyway… here's what I was saying. If you didn't help yourself there, nobody was going to give a damn about you. And nobody was going to help you. Nobody. I did what I had to do to stay alive. Nothing else. I had no reason to do something else. So this is what I did. What can I say? The guys liked me. Probably because I wasn't a typical *nudge* and I spoke good Polish."

Joe seemed a little defensive. I wasn't exactly sure why. It seemed to me that what he "did" was so far beyond reproach (as if reproaches belong anywhere near this discussion), and that, in fact, he used his advantage to help others survive. Spread the wealth, as it were.

"Joe, you don't have to justify or explain anything. Honestly. I find it just amazing how well you 'get' people, and that you were already able to do this when you were so young. I mean… seventeen. You were seventeen! Some people never figure out how to deal with other people."

He smiled.

"I know," he said, almost sheepishly. "But, here's the thing. It's simple. You go through life, you meet different people who come from different places and different circumstances. Some people are nice, some not. Some you love, some you hate. If you appreciate what others do for you, you're nice to them, too. Simple."

I nodded, an invitation to go on.

132

"Listen," he said, "you judge a person for what he does, how he acts, how he behaves. You figure, 'well, he's a nice man, he's smart, he's educated,' and you think he's a nice guy and you want to be a friend of his. Another guy who is none of these things, he doesn't know how to act, how to feel, you don't want to be in his company. One thing you have that nothing can take away from you is what you feel about yourself. *Versteht?* Whether you're bad or good—you know that for yourself—but that's also for me to judge."

Understood.

"So, Joe," I asked, "where do you think you learned all of this? How did you know how to do this? Was it your father who taught you?"

I so wanted it to be his father. Was already writing out the poignant father-passes-on-life-philosophy scene in my head.

"My father? My father? How could my father have taught me these things? He didn't have a chance to. He was dead too soon."

He snapped this last piece at me. It was the first and only time he showed the slightest bit of anger. *Of course. How could I have been so thoughtless?* A knot twisted in my stomach.

"Oh, Joe. I'm so sorry. That was really dumb. And cruel. I'm so sorry. I really should have thought harder before I asked that."

He softened.

"It's okay, sweetie. I know. Listen: No one taught me this, told me how to do any of this. Okay? It's like I told you before: when your life is at stake, 1…2…3, you do it. You just do it. You have to."

***

As intuitive as Joe's theory is that dwelling in the past, that nursing one's pain, that *kvetching* is counter-productive, a piece of me just wanted Joe to admit that he, too, has a soft spot for his own pain. Not to consign him to the ranks of the *kvetchers*, but because that also is intuitive: that, when it comes right down to it, no matter what defenses we put up against it, in unguarded moments the pain creeps back in.

In one conversation, as I listen to the recording, I hear myself pushing for this admission, my voice growing more incredulous and higher pitched the more he waves away my attempts to make him dwell, the more he insists that normal means not-dwelling.

Joe had just finished telling me that his survival had only to do with luck, nothing more.

I wasn't buying it.

"I have something I want to say back to that. Do you remember when you were telling me about being in Gestapo headquarters? You said, 'what was I going to do, stand there like a dummy?' *No.*" Joe chuckled at this, pleased with his comeback and that I'd captured it verbatim. "So you have an understanding that you did things that other people didn't do, that you made choices that other people didn't make. And it's uncomfortable to think like that because it suggests that you were responsible when other people weren't. But what do you do with that?"

Joe responded defensively, with that jab at the Czestochowa Society newsletter: "... It tells you right here... none of us was smarter than the others... it worked for me, that's all that counts... do you see what I mean? As long as you see it, that's all that matters."

"Yes, I do see. I do. But, there's something that's so... I don't even know how to say it... as you describe all of your experiences throughout all of this and then when you go to Israel, you're very clear that you have to be independent because you don't know who to trust... you have a very clear sense that you were on your own. And you must have had that sense while you were going through all of this, but I'm wondering if now, as you're trying to put it back together again, if you're trying to minimize that on some level. You know what I mean, almost as if you have a feeling that you shouldn't own the fact that you were entirely independent. You know? Does that make sense? And you know, I'm not trying to... there's just admiration there, there's no judgment, I'm just trying to get into your mind."

There was a pause, then a sigh, then a response that wasn't exactly an answer but wasn't a side-step, either.

"I had to do it, regardless. And I went and did it, because I figured that was the best way to do it. I didn't realize or sit down and wait and think should I do, should I not do...I didn't have time. Every minute was like, 'I'm going to be dead,' so I had to move fast. I had no choice. You have to do what you have to do."

Nowhere to go, and audibly flustered, I took another route.

"So this seems like a disjointed question, Joe, but so, in the moment, when you were there, you weren't thinking, you just acted, but now... you know... what do you dream about? That's one of the questions I wanted to ask you."

Classic academic move: when all else fails, pull out Freud.

"I don't dream. Honestly, I don't. Do you know why?" Joe asked.

"Because you don't get enough sleep?" I joked.

He laughed. "Yes I do. I get enough sleep. I go to bed every night by 12:00, so that's no problem."

"But you never have dreams?"

"Once in a while," he conceded.

"Do you ever have *recurring* dreams? Anything that ever just keeps coming back?"

"No."

"Never, never?"

"Never. I tell you why. Because I decided to live life like a normal person."

"But you can't control your dreams, Joe! You can't!"

"None. I tell you something." Then comes the "everybody's got their *pekl*" bit.

"I tell you what. If you've got several different pieces and somebody tells you to pick, you're going to pick yours every time. And that's good, because maybe somebody else's is worse than yours. So take yours and say goodbye. You have a right to cry, you have a right to think whatever you want, you have a right to do everything close. *By yourself.* You know

135

what I mean?"

I didn't, but answered, "I know exactly what you're saying, and this is going to sound like I'm arguing with you, but I can't believe you don't have dreams, in your very own... I mean, there's such a difference between doing what you're doing, protecting others and wanting them to live normal lives... but then there's the quiet time when you're alone with your own thoughts and your own demons, and it never, ever comes back?"

"Not as far as the Holocaust."

"Really??" The pitch of my voice was lower now, still incredulous, but as though worn down. "But do you have... I don't know... do you ever... are there other things that come up? I don't know?"

"I wouldn't let it happen."

"But you don't have control over your dreams. They just come."

"You know what? When I go to sleep, I sleep. I don't just lie there and close my eyes and wait to go back... you know... there. I don't. Uh-uh."

"You don't know how remarkable this is. You don't."

He shrugs, smiles, victorious.

"All right," I said, "I'll let you off the hook. I still don't believe you, but I'll let you off the hook."

In this relentless line of questioning I seem bent on extracting—what, exactly? An admission? Tears? Bitterness?

It's as if I needed him to experience his own catharsis. And I needed to witness it. So I didn't let him off the hook. Before he could speak, I cut him off, pressed one more time, a last-ditch effort to get him to admit to a fraught inner life.

"But, isn't there anything? I understand that, in terms of the Holocaust, you've decided that if you live there you're going to be sick. But, is there anything else in your life that you can think of that you find that you *do* dwell on, that you do find yourself coming back to? That sort of becomes a place for you to get strength or hope or comfort to think about that time?"

"Not really," he said, his intonation sounding very much like Mel Brooks. "I'll be honest. You know, there are people who lived in the camps, they dwell on it and dwell on it. What the hell is going on?! You're here, you have love, you have family. Don't make other people sick with what you went through. I never, I don't mention nothing. And that's the story. Never, never will I do it. I don't tell what was."

***

Freud would have zeroed in on those denials, on those protestations of "never." Maybe that's what I was doing, too, and that's why I pushed so hard. I hear echoes, now, of Wiesel's string of "nevers" in Joe's "never never will I do it"—unsettling in that this actually feels like a tirade against Wiesel. There's something of the linguistic component of Nietzsche's revaluation of all values here: as if Joe is retrieving the term from the abyss, reclaiming it for the purposes of saying "yes" to life. When I first heard them, though, I couldn't accept these protestations, because they fly in the face of my own coping mechanisms, which tend far more decidedly toward *kvetching*, I'm ashamed to say. It's the Yiddish variation on that timeless philosophical question: if you *kvetch* in private, does it still make you feel better? In my opinion, there's only one answer to this question. No. No. A thousand times no.

The essence, the *power*, of *kvetching*, it seems to me, lies in its communal nature.

Which is why I find Joe's stoicism, his ability to stand in his own skin, so breathtaking. And why I have so much trouble wrapping my head around his sense that his story would become an imposition on and burden to others. The extension of his *pekl* theory—not only do we all have our own baggage, we have no right to ask someone else to carry it:

"What am I going to do? Walk down the street saying, 'I'm a Holocaust survivor?' Hey, people got their own problems. You cannot tell me that people don't have any problems. Everybody has problems, and I'm going to tell them, 'I'm a survivor?'"

There are spaces in Joe's memories reserved for communal understanding, moments that capture how he felt in the company of others who carried *pekls* similar to his. But it is a space that he describes as necessarily non-verbal, as if to speak of suffering would mean giving in to hopelessness. When he described his experience in Santa Maria with the Jewish Brigade to me, for instance, Joe said this, looking almost wistful as he said it:

"It was like a vacation, it really was. It was so beautiful there, on the sea. Like being in a spa. I mean, it wasn't a *vacation,* obviously, most of us were orphans who had nowhere to go. But it was nice. We could think about anything we wanted there, and we wanted to think about the future."

"I'm trying to imagine what it would be like to be around so many people who went through such a horrible experience," I told him. "So many people who were feeling the same way together. Did you ever talk about it?"

"Every once in a while, I guess we would talk about the past, but we didn't dwell on it. No one ever got emotional about it. Nobody was better off than anybody else. There was no time for feeling sorry for ourselves."

"It's just an interesting thing to think about, you know? All of you there together, and yet you're completely alone. What did it feel like to be so alone? What were you thinking about?"

Joe looked at me, cocking his head a little as if he couldn't quite believe the denseness of my questions.

"You read the draft of my story. Right? You know, when I was on that truck? So what did I say about that?"

"You said you didn't have time to mourn."

"That's right. I had to make choices, and my choice was to live and not to die. Ever since then I've been alone. And you know what? I'm still alone. In that respect, I'm still alone. My family now is my family now. But my mother and father and my sisters were my first family. So you see, I'm still alive, and I'm still alone, any way you look at it. I'm happy. I'm most happy for my family, for my children, my grandchildren. But I would be very happy to have my first family. So actually what I have, I have one family that I lost and another family that I was given by God, or whatever, however you want to take it."

"But all of you must have been feeling something like this. Wouldn't it have helped to talk about it?"

In what must have been an act of willed patience, Joe replied:

"We didn't talk about it because we didn't need to talk about it. It was useless to repeat all that because we knew each one of us had something to tell you about how they came there, how they survived."

"So it was useless to talk."

"That's right," he said, humoring me. "But I'll tell you something.

Until today, I still have pictures of my father and mother together. I still have pictures of my sisters. I look at them every day and I still can't understand it. But you know what? Life goes on. In your mind, you can do whatever you want and feel whatever you want, but that's all you can do. It's been over 60 years and in my mind, it's like yesterday, but that's all I can do is look at the pictures, that's all I got left. Listen, everybody has their own baggage, so I just keep it to myself. I just keep it inside, because nobody really, truly, gives a shit. If I want to cry, I cry to myself, because the only one who really cares about it is me. You got it? *No one will ever really understand how I feel.* To lose a family—the only one who can do it, the only one who can know is the one who goes through it. So I just act how I act and know what I know and that's it. Am I right?"

***

I think about Joe sometimes with his photographs, imagine him sitting alone in his room or on his couch, a worn box beside him, crying softly at first, and then with abandon. I think about him locked in the prison of his own mind, his own memories, even as he is surrounded by the people who love him, respect him, adore him.

When I think of him this way, it's with a mixture of guilt and helplessness. I should leave him alone, let him be, give him the privacy to mourn in his own way. But I see him, his diminished eighty-eight year-old body hunched over his memories, and all I want to do is hug him. Because I also see him as a skinny fifteen year-old who just lost his father.

All I want to do is take away that boy's pain.

PART FOUR:
CONVERGENCE THEORY

ALONE

As I sit on my tattered couch and listen to the conversation Joe and I had about his time in Santa Maria, I realize I kept pushing him to talk about what it meant—means—to him that he is alone. The astounding thoughtlessness of that question—"What did it feel like to be so alone?"—jabs at me now when I hear myself ask it. It's obsessive, how I seem to want to get at the shades of his aloneness, the nuances, the details. And now I see how this obsession shows up in the way I've told Joe's story. It guides my wish to leave him in uncluttered silence in Gestapo headquarters. It shapes the way I convey his experience in Santa Maria. And it's here in this passage that describes Joe's first moments after he's lost his father:

> Joe was entirely alone now. He had just left his father's corpse, no time to say Kaddish, no time to mourn. Mourning would have to come later—or never come at all.
>
> Now he had to disappear. The trucks would be back soon. He stood for a moment in the blood-spattered road, surveying his surroundings and weighing his options, which were rather limited. A few yards away was an apartment building, one-story, with doors opening up to a central corridor. It looked deserted. Joe dashed to the entrance, then to a ladder and climbed up to the top. Here, above the apartments, he found an attic. Making his way quietly to the darkest corner, he sat down and tried to catch his breath. Knees bent, head crumpled between them, arms crossed over as if shielding himself from the bullets that had just killed his father, Joe wept silently. He was fully aware that anything other than silence would put him in danger; he was just as aware that, were he to allow himself to release the wails that were lodged in his throat, they might never stop. Then he would be lost. Not for the first time, but now, in the first hour of his imposed solitude, he recognized how closely silence and restraint are linked to preservation.

So much of the process of crafting Joe's story—The Suit—involved stitching and unstitching our conversations into narrative, finding ways to bring Joe's patterns of speech into the real-time action. In every word of this passage, I hear the conversation that shaped it.

The conversation that changed everything.

"Any way you look at it, I'm still alive and I'm still alone."

When Joe says this, his voice is clear, calm, it doesn't change in any noticeable way. No discernible anger or bitterness, this is just something he's come to live with, as much a part of him as his head or his heart.

"What I can't stop thinking about is this," I told him. "I'm thinking about how you have that experience in Santa Maria where everybody knows what you're going through because everybody's gone through it, and then you have the experience when you come to the US and you go to the *Oneg Shabbat* parties and that kind of thing, and this time, you're still not talking about it, but it's because nobody has had the kind of experience that you've had. There's no way that you can explain it. And it's a very different kind of silence. That's kind of what I'm interested in..."

"Yeah..." Joe said, getting exactly what I was going for. "Well, I came to the US, and that's a different story. You close one page and you open another."

"So, you're always alone, but the quality of your being alone changes."

"Always alone. I've been alone since I got out of that truck and I was supposed to be dead. Until then I had my father—you know that. But once I lost my father... ever since... I'm all alone, as far as my first family. But I have my wife, and my children and my grandchildren. You're in my heart just the same. That's right. You're in my heart the same."

"Thank you." I hear in my voice—in my surprised giggle—how taken aback I was that he should say this. How touched I was—am—that he would place me in his heart.

"Yeah, I mean, I can't know how you feel, but I always feel alone too."

"You do?" Joe sounds genuinely surprised.

"Yeah. I mean, it's a different kind of feeling, but it's at the core of who I am."

"Really??" Still surprised, but more and more animated and excited.

"You got the same? You do? You see? You feel the same way?"

"I do," I answered, a little timid. "I think... it has to do with my own relationship with my father. He was very... hard to explain."

"No, no you can tell me." Joe said.

"He was... troubled, and he had a lot of pain, and he never quite figured out how to fit into the world. And we were really close." The words were spilling out now.

"You were close with your father?"

"Yes. And when he died, it felt like the person who knew me the best..."

Joe cut me off, then finished my sentence just as I was going to.

"When he died, you felt like you lost everything."

"Um-huh."

"And you still feel like that."

"And there are people in my life now who never knew him and so I feel like they'll never really know me."

I had never said this out loud to anyone.

"But you still, but you still feel... but you still think of him."

"Every day."

"Well, that's the same... what did I tell you?"

"I know. I know."

I laugh a little. So does Joe.

"So you know how I feel, and you know how you feel. And you know that nobody, not even your husband, can take the place of your father. He's your husband, you have his children, this and that. But still, your father is closer to you. You know that?"

"Yes," I told him, feeling exposed. I *did* know that, but didn't think anybody else did. "It was 17 years already that he died. So, it's a long time."

"How old was he?"

"47."

"47?! 47??? Oh baby. Oh my God. What happened?"

"Cancer."

"Ah, *cancre*." This unexpected use of the French hits me somehow. The hard "c" sounds more at home in Joe's mouth. "Where?"

"Pancreatic."

147

"Oh, that's the biggie. That's the worst one. That's a shame."

"So, when I met you, I was working on a book about him. And then I met you and decided I wanted to work on you instead, and then I'll come back to him, because it's all connected. It's all very strange."

"So you see," Joe said, "we have a lot together. Very much. 47. My God. The fact is, he died so young. Was he sick a long time?"

"No, he found out in July and he died in January."

"So, six months?"

"Yep."

"Your mother didn't get remarried, did she?"

This time, as I listen, I hear his concern for my mother, and his assumption that she and my father must have been in love. The benefit of the doubt.

"She and my father got divorced when I was a year and a half."

"A year and a half before he died?"

"No, when I was a baby. My mom married my stepfather when I was eight."

"And he's good to you, your stepfather?"

"Yes, very good. He's a very good man. I'm very close to him. My father didn't do any of the kinds of things fathers are supposed to do... and, so, my stepfather did everything for me... put me through college... everything."

"That's nice."

"Yes. But still, he's not my father."

"I know," Joe said, concurring. "I know I know I know. I know. I'm there, right?"

So right.

"I know. And it's not the same. It's a very different situation, but there's a kind of way..."

"That's right, it's not the same," Joe said, but not in a way that discounted or minimized or put me in my place. He continued, "But you've got to live with it. And here you met me. And I've got you."

"Yep. And somewhere I think my father's smiling about all of this." Laughing.

"I'm telling you, life... plays different tricks," Joe, chuckling softly, shaking his head.

"It sure does."

"It plays different tricks. Let me ask you a question. When you met me, the first time... what did you think?"

The question embarrassed me. It felt too intimate. But I answered him honestly, conspiratorially, even.

"I felt immediately like you were familiar, like I knew you. I knew we were going to get along. I don't know how the rest of your family feels about me, but I knew we were going to get along."

"Look. You and I, I and you, nobody else. Okay? We have the same. Your father passed away, I lost my father. You see? Poor baby, you didn't get a chance to be with your father very much."

"Well, they were 20 very powerful years. I was 20 when he died."

"Twenty?"

"Yeah, we spent a lot of time together. He was very... I think I told you this... that's why I'm so drawn to you. Because you are the opposite of everything that he did. He did everything the wrong way. He was very... he just, he couldn't... he didn't live the right way. And he never felt like he could, and he was always breaking the rules, and breaking the law and... um...," I clear my throat, "breaking people's hearts."

"Really? He had some other women on the side?"

"I think he did, when he was married to my mom. I don't know if he did or not. I'm pretty sure he did, but he abused her, and he was horrible to her. He was very, very horrible to her. But he was the kind of person who was very charismatic, and so you were drawn to him, and then he played his mind-games with you. And, he was very... do you know anybody like that? That's what he was like. So, it was hard to know what the truth was, because he kept turning it around. And you just wanted to believe him so badly."

"He wouldn't tell you the truth?"

Joe seemed genuinely surprised that a father could be a liar.

"He would tell me versions of the truth. And some things he would tell me were true. Others weren't. Yeah, he was just a very... interesting... person, because I never doubted that he loved me, or that he was who he thought he was. He just couldn't, you know... some people can't... live. They can't find a way to do it. And *you*," my voice changes here, becomes more energetic, "are completely the opposite." I pause.

149

"*You're* a survivor. You… are a true survivor."

"I tell you as it is."

"He squandered his life."

"I tell you as it is."

"Um-huh."

"I don't lie to you."

"Nope."

"And I don't want you to lie to me, either."

"Yeah, I don't lie."

"I know."

"Because of him."

"I know. I don't want you to lie."

"No." A promise.

"No. Ah, baby. Yep. I'm telling you… life is… you never know."

I hear him patting my hands.

"You never *do* know." Laughing.

"You never know. Yep. I like it this way."

"Me too," I say, brightly.

"I like it this way."

Curled up on that tattered couch in Brunswick, Maine, listening to the recording. I felt emptied out. Hollow. It was my own catharsis I had witnessed.

****

January 27, 1992. My father had died hours earlier, his body lingering in the living room several hours more before the funeral parlor finally came to pick him up. For the first hour or so, my brother and I played at being morose, solemn, torn apart, but we were really more self-conscious about how we were supposed to behave in the presence of this dead body that had just recently been our dad. As the hours passed and the situation began to seem more and more absurd, we cracked nervous jokes, for my father's benefit. He would have been self-conscious, too. He would have cracked jokes, too, more tasteless than any of ours.

That night I lay in the bathtub, submerged to my neck, contemplating my 20-year-old body in a way that was strangely dissociated, if not exactly numb.

This is a fatherless body.

I pulled my head under the water, to magnify or drown out the thought that had come into it, fully formed. Eyes squeezed shut, lips and fists clenched, violently refusing to see or speak this new reality. I don't know how long I stayed like this.

Lifted my head out. Needing to breathe. Needing to sob.

One nearly-primal scream.

Then panic.

****

I have a theory that helps me understand my interactions with the people I care most about. It's the theory of convergence, the idea that we meet the people we most need to meet when we're most open to meeting them. Our paths converge, in other words. It's not exactly fate. It's not that our paths *have to* converge. It's more that *we need* them to converge when they do and the weight of our need swerves our paths together.

The Yiddish term for this is *beshert*. It generally has to do with finding your soulmate. The term comes from the German word meaning "given," as in God-has-given-you-this-person-to-complete-you. *Beshert* also comes from the Yiddish term for "scissors." As in, this person has been cut from cloth to fit you. Part-Jewish, part-Plato, part-Jerry Maguire, it's every romantic fantasy wrapped into one. God-as-tailor references aside, what I latch onto is the image of the scissors, the blades, the sharpness, the being torn open, cut apart. What I latch onto is the richness and paradox of these varied derivations existing together: gift, completion, artistry, cutting apart.

My experience with Joe has been a magic ride of convergence, of *beshert*. I sensed it from the very beginning, the moment I saw him. I think Joe sensed it, too.

"It's like I told you," Joe said once. "Everybody has their story. And no two stories are alike. That's my story, and that's yours. And the two meet or not. And we meet. We meet, we met, and we shall meet, forever and ever. Don't you leave me."

Joe's "don't you leave me" tears at me, cuts me apart. This has been my longtime silent mantra, as I watch my boys sleep, as I curl into my husband in our bed, as I witness my mother's memory slip away. I know the fear of that phrase, the terror that attachment brings.

On the other side of that mantra is grace—for having been gifted attachments so strong I can't bear to have them broken. It's grace I feel most strongly when Joe says we're the same because we both lost our fathers. It's grace I feel that he sees and calls my father's death a shame, when so many others have seen it as a blessing in disguise. It's grace—that he who lost so much should cut through to the quick of it, finishing my sentences, recognizing my pain as like his own.

I just forced myself to re-read "Daddy." My reaction to the poem is too strong for me not to know that something's buried down deep that's worth uncovering. I hurled some pretty mean insults and accusations at Sylvia, which I'm feeling guilty about. She probably doesn't deserve them. If she does, then I might need to hurl them at myself, too. Even if she doesn't, I might need to.

There's one line I keep seeing in the poem now. One little line that everything seems to swirl around.

"Ich, ich, ich, ich," she says. "I, I, I, I."

Most of my anger is directed at Sylvia for what I've named narcissism, self-absorption. And here I have the string of first person pronouns to prove it. But I'm self-aware enough to worry that, if she's a self-absorbed narcissist, well, maybe I am too.

These are the things I worry about when I think about how to tell Joe's story, despite Joe's unerring graciousness:

- That I've co-opted Joe's story by placing my own story alongside of it.
- That it is inappropriate to bring my own "daddy" into this.
- That I have allowed my conversations with Joe—which were supposed to be about collecting the details of *his* story—to veer at times into territory that has more to do with me than him.
- That I've exploited Joe by sharing some of the more intimate details of these conversations.

When I'm screaming at Sylvia, what I'm really doing is trying to drown out that voice in my head: have I made this storytelling all about me? Is it okay to tell Joe's story the way I've chosen to tell it, with my big old "Ich" intruding in every which way?

There are *rules* about how to write about the Holocaust—written and unwritten, inviolable. There must be, or Sylvia wouldn't make me so angry and I wouldn't feel so anxious about the prospect of being just like her. Rule number one: the only "I" who can speak about these things is the person who went through it. And rule number two: the thing written about has to be True, with a capital T—no room for literary embellishment, no room for metaphorical/allegorical analogies, no room for imagining, say, the kind of character Sylvia places at the center of her poem.

When Joe and I were in the midst of our meetings, news broke that Herman Rosenblat's Holocaust memoir, *Angel at the Fence*,[29] touted by Oprah Winfrey as "the single greatest love story" she'd ever heard, was fabricated.[30] Not the whole memoir, apparently, but the part that gives the book its title: Herman made up the bit about the woman—who later becomes his wife— who threw apples to him over the fence at Schlieben, a sub-camp of Buchenwald. When I asked Joe what he thought about that, he said—spat, really—"That guy is a MORON. A real moron. People believed in him. He ruined it for himself." Joe places a premium on truth. "I tell it as it is," he says. And he does, no bells and whistles. Just the facts, ma'am.

And it has to be this way. It has to be, if Holocaust memoirs are intended as historical documents. And they are, primarily. Holocaust historian Deborah Lipstadt sums up powerfully the stakes of Rosenblat's fabrication in her article, "A Danger Greater than Denial":

> *I have spent much of my academic career studying Holocaust denial. But the much greater danger to our collective memory of the event is posed by Holocaust trivialization and romanticization. What the Rosenblats and their enablers did was create yet another obstacle for the remaining survivors to convince others that their stories are true.*
>
> *Rosenblat claims that all he wanted to do was make people love each other more. The Chabad rabbi [who read the memoir, was taken in by it, and performed a belated Bar Mitzvah for Rosenblat] probably thought the story would inspire faith. Salomon [who is making a film of the memoir] wanted to teach Middle America about the Holocaust.*
>
> *These may be worthy goals. But the Holocaust should not be reduced to a means for trying to fulfill these or any other ends. The instrumentalization of the Holocaust, the use of it to fulfill something else, is the ultimate degradation of the event.*[31]

I'm pretty sure this is what Joe was going for by his more succinct use of the term "moron."

There was a time in my life when I pored over Deborah's book, *Denying the Holocaust*,[32] filling the margins with notes and exclamations, shaken to the core to learn that there was such a thing as Holocaust denial and that people could express it so... diabolically. It's because I respect her work so much that I hear that term "trivialization" and those last two sentences as a personal reprisal. Am I trivializing? Am I reducing the Holocaust to a means for trying to fulfill my own ends (with the "ends" being figuring out why the heck my father keeps popping in and out of my conversations with Joe)?

This, in a nutshell, is what I'm so anxious about.

But let me just play this through. What Deborah says here travels in a Holocaust Studies neighborhood that makes a similar—and rather standard—argument. It is this argument I keep hearing in my head alongside of those anxieties that I like to project onto Sylvia. The term is "uniqueness," and it goes something like this: The Holocaust presents a unique, singular, irreproducible historical moment. The factors in play—political, cultural, economic, theological, geographical—collided and colluded in a perfect storm that had never been seen before and has not been seen since. Given its uniqueness, it is impossible to compare to other genocides and to the crimes against humanity displayed in the midst of these genocides. This argument gets played out on the individual level as well; if the Holocaust represents a unique event, so too, the suffering of individuals in the midst of this event is unique, incomparable to other kinds of suffering.

I have made this argument, on most of its levels, on a number of occasions. In graduate seminars, for instance, I self-righteously pulled out the Holocaust trump card when I was the only Jew in the room, in what now appears to me as an act of either perceived self- or collective-defense. I recognize the warning at the center of the argument: to compare is to diminish. It is an act of audacity, a symbolic act of violence, degradation, to claim to know and to understand pain of this magnitude. It is an insult to presume that we can ever really know what another person has experienced. It is more compassionate to acknowledge how wide the gap is between you and me than it is to attempt to bridge this gap with false equivalencies.

The reason the argument for uniqueness resonates with me is because it validates my own gut-level feeling that something unprecedented, something profoundly—other—happened during the Holocaust. It also resonates because it is so well-intentioned; it is meant to protect survivors from those who might capitalize on their pain or hurt them with their thoughtlessness. This same protective spirit is all over Deborah's response to Herman Rosenblat, and that is why her way of seeing things makes so much sense to me.

But, there's something about Deborah's use of the term "collective memory" that nags at me, the closer I get to Joe. It's a practical statement that makes perfect sense coming from an historian: we *must* learn, collectively, the objective truth of what happened during the Holocaust. But I'm starting to wonder if there really is such a thing as collective *memory*. Joe's memories are not collective. They're his and his alone. When Joe goes into that space of specified memory—when he looks at his pictures and remembers faces and names and spaces and events and... midnight blue bicycles—I *can't* see the things he's seeing. What I can see is the *effect* these non-communicable specifics have on him. What I can do is imagine what he is seeing and try to enter into his world. What I can do is make a connection between his mental images, the effects of those images, and the ones that are swirling around in my own brain as a result of my own experiences.

Maybe this is all an elaborate rationalization of that dreaded self-absorption I keep worrying about. Maybe. But something in me feels like this connection-making is the thing that I can do to protect Joe from becoming the guy on stage on Holocaust Remembrance Day that people, despite themselves, stop listening to.

I'm taking my cues from Joe now. And these cues don't translate neatly into answers to the is-there-such-a-thing-as-collective-memory or is-it-possible-to-compare-non-Holocaust-suffering-to-Holocaust-suffering sorts of questions. Joe told me (at least) two things that seem like they should be mutually exclusive, like they should cancel each other out:

1)   If I want to cry, I cry to myself, because the only one who really cares about it is me. No one will ever really understand how I feel.

2)   You and I, I and you, nobody else. Okay? We have the same. Your father passed away, I lost my father. You see?

But they *don't* cancel each other out. They are *both* true, simultaneously. Joe's taught me that the rules of engagement are, in fact, *messy*. And contradictory. And irrational. And sometimes, yes, sometimes, self-absorbed. Those academic arguments, well-intentioned though they are, don't take the messiness of human interaction into account. They don't capture the fact that the conversations Joe and I share express hope and despair and disappointment and humor and frustration and transcendence and ambivalence (sometimes in the same minute). They don't seem to allow for the possibility of a relationship. Instead, they seem to lead back to that stage, engulfing and enshrining that poor speaker in his aloneness, his uniqueness.

****

In the last minute of that long conversation I had with Joe about my not-going to the camps, I said to him:

"I think it's good for us to have this conversation. I think our conversation here… what you're trying to get me to struggle with and what I'm trying to get you to struggle with is part of what people will be interested in, if that makes any sense. I think it's… both of us together…"

"We click," Joe laughed.

"Yes, that's right. We click. You're very important to me."

"It's very important to me, too, to click with you. Because, I, eh, you are in my life. How's that? You are in my life forever. I feel, ever since we started, I feel better and better. I see you better. Because it takes time to really get together, to click. And the more I see you, the more I feel you, you understand?

"I do. I feel the same way."

"And there's nothing you can take away from me. You are you, and I am me, and nothing will change that. Because we have built very good feelings. Okay? I love you."

"I love you, too."

This last minute of the conversation—it also felt like grace.

****

The first time I read "Daddy," it wasn't actually the Holocaust representation stuff that made me want to smack Sylvia. That came later. What came first was the rage—yes, rage—I felt at these lines: "Daddy, I have had to kill you," "So, daddy, I'm finally through," which eventually culminate in this stanza:

There's a stake in your fat black heart
And the villagers never liked you.
They are dancing and stamping on you.
They always *knew* it was you.
Daddy, daddy, you bastard, I'm through.

The first time I read this poem, my father was still very much alive, still very much wreaking his own personal brand of havoc, which expressed itself in my unconscious in a recurring dream I had from the time I was about eight until he died.

In the dream, I ran and ran, barefoot, in light pajamas just barely protecting me from the dewy night, zigzagging my way through trailer parks and tenement houses, stumbling and falling, painfully, blindly, as my father chased me with a machete, screaming obscenities that would later come to signal love. He never caught me.

In *that* dream, he never caught me. There was one night, though, when the scene had shifted. This time we were in a glittering penthouse, and I was trapped by the height and the floor-to-ceiling windows all around. My father stood by the window, calm, confident, impeccable in a suit, holding a gun. He aimed it at my head, preceding the shot with all-too-transparent remark: "I have to kill you. I have to kill you because I love you so much." One shot and it was over.

So, you see, Sylvia's not the only one with daddy issues that express themselves violently. I should have been able to commiserate with her. I should have admired her for taking the bull by the horns, as it were, driving the stake into the heart of her father's memory, killing him off once and for all.

Instead, her brutality horrified me. Her joy in collaborating with those laughing, dancing, grave-stomping villagers repulsed me. How could she do this? How could she say these things about her father? Her *daddy*? The first time I read this poem, I was a college student, and I was in a class with others who seemed entirely unruffled by her words. I remember sitting there, shaking, blind with anger—at Sylvia, at my classmates, at the professor, who was blissing-out in a Freudian reverie about the power that comes in the sexualizing and subsequent killing off of the father. How could they not see it? This was *wrong*. Sylvia violated a basic human code: she desecrated her father. In writing. For all the world to see.

The literature professor in me now just shakes her head at my naiveté, then rushes off to grab a cup of coffee with the other professor to continue the conversation. After all, this is the essence of what good literature does. It unsettles. It disrupts. It pisses people off. It gives you the occasion to talk about Freud (or Lacan, if you're into that kind of thing).

But the student-me stays behind, still chilled by Sylvia's defiant murder of her father—even if it was only symbolic, even if it was only a dramatization, even if it was only an allegory. And the adult-me, who now reads this poem in the shadow of my father's long-ago death and in the presence of Joe, joins her, still angry, but with a sharper sense of focus.

I hear Joe saying to me—"So you know how I feel, and you know how you feel, and you know that *nobody* can take the place of your father." I hear him saying these things even after he learns more about my father's questionable way of being in the world. I hear the pain in his voice the day I was thoughtless enough to ask him if he'd learned the art he has for reading people, one of his key survival strategies, from his father: "My father? My father? How could my father have taught me these things? He didn't have a chance to. He was dead too soon." I hear these things and it now occurs to me that my anger is directed more at what seems to be Sylvia's profound lack of gratitude, her profound lack of respect for the time she did have with her father. I am angry with her for her unwillingness to express the death of her father as loss. She could have done that even as she danced on his grave.

All of this is crazy on my part. I do know that. It is crazy to get this hung up on a poem, to carry around this anger at the person who created it. Especially because I do know a bit about Sylvia's history and the experiences that led her to write this poem. It's painful stuff. And it's *her* poem to write, after all. Who am I to judge her for expressing her pain in the way she chooses to express it?

But I *am* judging her. I'm judging her because she has insulted Joe and me with the cavalier and cold-blooded way she has cast aside her father. I'm judging her because she implicitly makes the statement that it is possible to move on from the death of your father, that it is possible to feel anything other than ripped to pieces by it, that it is possible not to mourn.

I don't *want* to be "through" with my father. I don't *want* to kill him off.

And I know it's self-absorbed, and I fear it is probably narcissistic, but I feel like Joe has told me I don't have to.

The Things He Carried

*O*nce, when I was in the eighth grade, shoulders stooped and cringing with shame at my own glaring inadequacies, all wistful and unreciprocated and unnamable desire for romance, I sat with my father in the cold and the dark on the beach.

"Beppers," he said (his pet name for me), "look at that sky, just look at it. There's so much in that sky, so many possibilities. Don't you ever, ever, let anyone tell you that you need to follow a certain path. I know you're hurting and confused right now, and feeling like the world is pulling you in a million different directions, and that your mother and I are pulling you in a million more. I know you're not really sure of your place in all of this. I know you don't really feel like you have much to offer, and you can't quite be sure that you fit in. But, kid, let me tell you something: you're going to figure it out, you're going to find your way. You're a Harrison, and that means that you've got this inner strength that's going to guide you, it's going to allow you to make choices without compromising your integrity. And, for what it's worth, you do have something to offer: you make me proud, just being my daughter. You and your brother are the only thing I've ever done right."

There, in that place that belonged to no one else but us (because no one cared to claim it), we contemplated the largeness of the universe. There, with generosity and intuition, my father transformed the threat of that largeness, its imposition and demands, into a mystery waiting to be unraveled. I have no idea how and where he came to such a conclusion about the essential nobility of the Harrison character (much objective evidence... and witnesses... could convincingly protest against this conclusion), but his words, however self-congratulatory and delusional, comforted me. He comforted me, not with easy answers or platitudes, but with an honest acknowledgment that life is hard, that it can't be easily navigated, that "figuring it out" means less about reducing things to their simplest components than it does watching complexity multiply. My father, a pathological liar according to the most basic rules of social acceptability, remained fiercely honest and consistent in this piece of advice he gave me here and on so *many other occasions (not always as benign as this one): look pain directly in the face. Know it, know its source, and embrace it. Because it is in pain that we find strength. It is in complexity and difficulty that we see what we're made of.*

This scene came from that manuscript I was working on about my dad, "Prodigal Father," before I met Joe. When I read it now, I feel exposed and vulnerable, embarrassed, caught in a moment of self-indulgence. Like a little girl playing dress up with her fancy thesaurus. O'Brien, again, creeps up on me, and his distinction between story truth and happening truth. And it seems to me that, as much as the details I provide capture the "truth" of what *happened*, the overall scene doesn't ring true, doesn't have the sharp clarity of my memory of that night on that beach. It also feels too insular, too self-referential—just me sitting in a hall of mirrors.

But still, I feel attached to these paragraphs. Mainly because I feel attached to the memory that inspired them. And I wonder: is this *my* midnight-blue racing bike? Is this a memory that is at once so specific to me and so foundational for the story I'm trying to tell that it both can't and must be woven into the mix?

I think about the spilling out of memory, about the way Joe's box of pictures spills out, uncontained, all over the table between us. I think about how different this is from him sitting alone with those pictures— how that table between us now renders this a communal act, a space where he can share his memories, even if he can't fully communicate the universe of meaning behind them. He picks up a picture randomly or seeks it out deliberately. Either way, the thread of the story he goes on to tell starts there, with that picture that means something only to him, until he tells me what it means.

****

My father died with virtually nothing to his name.

The things he carried were random and arbitrary: a closetful of clothes; assorted housewares (circa 1970s); a rotary phone burned in an office fire, plastic roiling, puckering and settling into a coffee-table curiosity; a box full of photo albums and reel-to-reel films (no projector); a plastic green file folder including: a (poetically altered) resume; an acceptance letter to law school; a mock letter of recommendation written by a partner at the law firm for which he worked as a paralegal; three real letters of recommendation; homemade cards and drawings from my brother and me; random court papers and post-divorce letters from my mom.

I found a good number of these things in boxes that had been moved countless times from apartments to storage units and back again, round and round and round, eventually landing in my friend's basement (his mom had let my father store them there), to collect dust.

The rest of the things, my dad left behind in his fiancée's house, the house where he died after several months of hospice care. She gave me these things, and now I carry them.

Picture them spilling out onto the table between us.

CRAIG HARRISON
140 E. Georgianna Drive
Richboro, PA 18954

JOB OBJECTIVE
Career sales/marketing management position leading to senior management.

BUSINESS EXPERIENCE

1976 to Present MOTIVATORS, INC. Philadelphia, PA
Principal/Management Consultant. Responsible for sales and marketing consulting with companies which are primarily dealers and manufacturer representatives of commercial and industrial electronic, mechanical, chemical and computerized products. Managerial duties include establishing and maintaining new and existing client dealerships, agents and product lines; developing, implementing and monitoring all related sales and marketing management and consulting functions for dealer personnel, agents, and company sales and marketing representatives. Began as a sales and marketing representative selling products and services to new and existing accounts.

1973 to 1976 IBM CORPORATION Cherry Hill, NJ
Marketing Representative. Responsible for the sales of IBM's office products in Cape May and Atlantic Counties, New Jersey. Attained a superior sales record with sales in excess of 200% in each product line. Received IBM's Man of the Month 7 of 12 months, and Rookie Salesman of the Year in District 20 and the Eastern Region during the 1973-74 selling year. In 1974-75 selling year, sales in excess of 240% in each product line. Received IBM's Man of the Month Award 10 of 12 months. Returned to the training facility on two occasions as the head sales training instructor; and on three occasions as an industry marketing coordinator.

1970-1973 NATIONAL SPINNING COMPANY Washington, NC
Department Head, dye winding department, reporting to Plant Manager. Duties included supervision of eighty employees from machine operators to maintenance personnel to foremen. Scheduled production, responsible for troubleshooting, coordinated production with key marketing and sales functions. Began as Executive Trainee, with exposure to all facets of the business.

1964-1967 SEARS, ROEBUCK AND COMPANY St. Davids, PA
Display Department. Initial assignment in individual department displays; Subsequently assumed complete responsibility for ten departments. Scheduled display production and setups, coordinated displays with individual and storewide promotions. Left to attend college full-time.

TEACHING EXPERIENCE

1981 to Present COMMUNITY COLLEGE OF PHILADELPHIA
Part-time instructor. Teaching all business related subjects.

EDUCATION

1967 to 1970 PHILADELPHIA COLLEGE OF TEXTILES AND SCIENCES
Bachelor of Science Degrees. Business Management and Marketing; and Textile Engineering, Management and Marketing.

1981-1985 Master in Business Administration, Finance, Management and Marketing. While an undergraduate, member of the American Marketing Association, Delta Sigma Pi Professional Business Fraternity, Marketing Club, Computer Club, and Varsity Baseball team. College and living expenses 100% financed through summer and part-time employment of over 35 hours/week.

MILITARY SERVICE

1965-1971 United States Army Reserve. Transportation Company. Honorably discharged with rank of second lieutenant. Six months active duty for training served in 1965.

REFERENCES Personal references will be forwarded upon request.

This is how my father saw himself, or better, how he packaged himself for others. Pretty funny stuff, in how little it resembles actual reality. As I sit looking at this resume, I wonder how much of this he believed, how much is simple wish-fulfillment, how much is deliberate deception. Motivators, Inc. was my grandfather's company. The only real attachment my dad had to it was by blood and this paragraph he concocted to account for his whereabouts over the course of the eleven years that passed between his last "management" position (also doctored quite poetically) and the writing of this resume. As far as military service goes, the movie "Stripes" (one of my father's all-time favorites) *before* Bill Murray gets his act together is closer to the truth; here he significantly upgrades the six weeks basic training he (barely) completed to six years of service ending in an honorable discharge with rank of second lieutenant. Ha! That's a good one!

Other details are also fudged significantly and/or necessarily omitted: his tenure with National Spinning Company was one year, not three; his employment with IBM and Sears ended abruptly when charges of stealing equipment and sexually harassing the women subordinate to him were brought against him. Ugh. All evidence of his stint at my grandfather's shop—to the tune of $30,000 embezzled (my grandfather never pressed charges)—is entirely erased. With a push of a typewriter key, gone. It never existed.

I have had quite a relationship with this piece of paper over the years. The first time I saw it, it made me angry. I took it as a personal insult that he went out of his way to depict on paper a guy who anyone would respect. It was as if he wanted to give us a glimpse into what he thought was our unvoiced hopes, as if he wanted to call our attention to all the potential he squandered. As if he wanted to acknowledge that he knew exactly the kind of man others wished he would be, and then deliberately refused to be this man.

Later, I got sad. I thought about him going through the process of putting these words on paper, about him coming face to face with the man he easily could have become but, for reasons I'll never fully be able to understand, didn't. What must he have felt when he came face to face with this man? When he looked in the mirror, did he believe his own lies, or did he feel defeated by how far he missed the mark he set for himself?

Now, as I might have already given away, I find this piece of paper pretty amusing. Now, as I look at it, I'm rooting for my father to convince people that he is this guy he claims to be. The balls on this guy, the chutzpah! If I feel sadness now in looking at this, it has more to do with the fact that my brother and I never really did want him to be the man he depicted on this piece of paper, and if he *did* beat himself up over not being this man, it would have been wasted energy. The paper successes, the credentials meant nothing to us. What we loved was the way he defied the rules, the magic he made, his refusal to do things the way everybody else was doing them. Why couldn't he put *those* skills on a resume?

When I look at this creative self-portrait now, I see, curiously, a guy who looks very much like Joe: a self-made man who dutifully serves his country, puts himself through college, and earns praise and recognition as a businessman and an athlete. Beyond all this, I see a man who knew who he needed to be in order to play the game.

Excerpts from "The Suit"

**

"And you snuck into Rakow?" Something like admiration was unmistakable in Miloff's face.

"Yes, sir."

"Why?"

Then Joe did lie, but convincingly enough to charm Miloff and save himself:

"Because I want to work for you, sir," he told him. "I want to contribute to your efforts. Your country. Your government." He laid it on thick.

Miloff knew he was being charmed, but at this point didn't seem to mind. This kid impressed him…

**

"I'm Klobucki now," Joe said to himself as soon as he had his bearings in the Rakow barracks. Miloff hadn't written his name down; there were no records of a Joseph Koenigheit at the camp, and Joe wanted to keep it that way…

At this point, the name change was largely symbolic, a security measure so that, when he would need to assume a new identity—in places where it would mean certain death to be a Jew—he would have it ready at his fingertips. Insurance against the fatal condition of being caught off-guard or flustered. In the relative protection of this place and in the privacy of his own head, he tried on this typical Polish name, testing its fit against his Jewish skin. He was surprised how little it chafed against him, necessity apparently diminishing his attachment to his own name.

**

Joe learned quickly that connections were everything here. A kibbitzer by nature, a people person, Joe leaned heavily into it now, in single-minded pursuit of friendship with the blocowy and his assistants. It wasn't hard to come by; the blocowy enjoyed talking with Joe and took an instant liking to him.

****

The thing about my father is that he had his heroes. Real people, models he could aspire to. And he had no problem telling his heroes how he felt about them, he never played coy games to hide his feelings or protect himself. I saw how he talked to his heroes when the senior lawyer of the firm my dad worked for sent me copies of letters my dad had written to him and to another lawyer right before he died.

In these letters, he not only names these two men as "role models" and "guiding lights" but also lists the specific actions they have taken to achieve this status for him. It's as though he is providing a blueprint for his own personal code of ethics at the same time that he pinpoints exactly what he was unable to accomplish: "you do things on the up and up, no cutting corners," "you're a good father and husband and you take good care of your family," "I so admire and envy your ability to see things as you do and react as you do to the pressures of life. You take care of your family and despite your grumblings, you're always there for them." Loyalty, perseverance, selflessness, level-headedness, being a good father and husband: qualities that he could so easily and generously identify as qualities worth striving for. Qualities he could both admire and envy. Qualities he couldn't enact, no matter how hard he may have wanted to enact them.

I find myself wondering about what it means that my father, himself so un-heroic, should have been so quick to name his heroes. Maybe it is actually the natural consequence of self-awareness, of knowing who he was, who he could never be, and who he might like to become if he could have somehow managed to get out of himself long enough to accomplish all those things so counter to his nature. If so, there is something inherently self-deprecating in the act of hero worship—a conscious admission that my hero embodies something I lack.

When I read these letters again now, I think about the day I told Joe about my father. The day I made that tentative admission that I also feel alone. I think about how I felt in that split second when Joe assumed that my father was still happily married to my mom when he died, the briefest moment of fantasy that I allowed myself to see my father through Joe's lens of fatherhood and family—before correcting his

170

assumption. What I felt in that moment was something like what I felt the first time I saw my father's doctored resume: wistfulness, longing for the man my dad couldn't be.

But these letters offer the possibility for another fantasy that I'd much rather think about...

I imagine my father still alive and well and accompanying me to my meetings with Joe. I imagine introducing them, with Joe having prior knowledge of his shenanigans. Then I imagine Joe slapping him up one side of his head and down the other. He wouldn't be yelling—that's not Joe's style—but he would be angry, and he would make it clear in no uncertain terms that he'd better get his act together. He'd call him out for being a liar and a shitty father and husband and he'd tell him to cut it out, for god's sake, and *be a man*.

And because my father would have the same picture in his mind of what that meant, of what that man should look like, he'd take it, every bit of it, without even attempting to argue. He'd nod, ashamed, with full recognition that he'd been rightfully told off. But alongside that shame would be admiration, and respect, and gratitude—the kind of hero's welcome that he felt so comfortable giving.

****

Of all the things he carried, which I now do, my favorite is an extra large black t-shirt embroidered with the initials F.Y.I.Y.C.T.A.J. Know what it stands for?

FUCK YOU IF YOU CAN'T TAKE A JOKE

This was my father's battle-cry, his all-purpose put-down/pep-talk (in this last form, it morphed into "Fuck *them* if they can't take a joke," firmly cementing the distinction between "us" and "them" that he lived by). I got him this t-shirt one year for his birthday, mighty pleased with myself as I marched up to the kiosk in the mall with my crumpled money and cryptic initials. My dad was pleased, too, giving me a thumbs-up when he opened it.

Now, I want to dig into it, this t-shirt slogan become battle-cry. Now I wonder: What are the possible responses to a joke a person doesn't get or can't take? Silence, or confusion, or anger, insult, offense. Maybe the joke makes no sense; it's so bizarre you have no response. Or maybe you get the joke, but it leaves you flat or pisses you off. In any case, *fuck you* is a pretty extreme thing for the guy who made the joke to say. *Fuck you*, after all, is the insult of last resort, the thing you shout at your lover just before you slam the door. It's the breaking point, the explosion of accumulated hurt, anger, disappointment. You don't just bounce back from *fuck you*—whether you're on the giving or receiving end.

If I don't get your joke, it's not that I'm actively pushing you away. We just didn't connect. If I *can't take* your joke, it's personal. It may be a result of my own incapacity (*can't*), but now I'm refusing to enter into your game. Now I'm rejecting you. And depending on the stakes of your game, my refusing to enter into it may in fact merit a *fuck you*.

I see now why my father loved the phrase so much. It's the same reason I love it so much. It's so rich; there are so many levels when you start turning it over and over. First, there's the fact that someone who uses this phrase takes on the role of a person whose world others cannot enter. There's rawness in this role, vulnerability, a willingness to make oneself vulnerable, a willingness to reject propriety for its own sake. In other words, the guy saying this isn't trying to win any diplomacy awards; he's letting it all hang out, telling you how he feels.

But there's also a kind of one-two punch going on, a classic reversal, a way of moving past the vulnerability to a place of strength. It's a way of saying: I, the person hurling the f-bomb at you, might be the joker, but you, my friend, *you're* the joke. You're the one who can't see clearly. You're the one who takes everything so damn seriously. Or maybe it's that you don't take things seriously *enough*. Or that you don't take the *right things* seriously.

The phrase spins out its own little cautionary tale: those people who can't take a joke are so busy living their lives according to a set of pre-determined rules that they have no chance for self-reflection, no chance to look deeply into things.

That day in the Corner Bakery, when Joe smiled that toothy smile across the table at me as I argued for the expletive-laden version of the chapter of him refusing to be bullied, I heard this phrase behind that smile. My hearing it gave me the strength to keep going and to push harder to represent Joe as honestly as I could. My takeaway lesson from my deconstruction of this phrase is not so much that it's reactionary (though it can be read this way) as that it's a call to make meaning, specifically, by taking things simultaneously more and less seriously. "Lighten up," my father would say to me on so many occasions. I felt defeated when he said this, but I think he really meant to energize me. *Don't be one of those people who can't take a joke*, he was saying. And he was right to say it.

In the retroactive way of so much memory-making, an image of Joe at that table dwarfed in this oversized black t-shirt flashes across my mind.

And it makes me smile.

****

The day Joe and I talked about the camps—about my not-going to them, to be more precise—things got intense. I wrote about it earlier as if his saying "I love you" and my saying it back was the culmination of the conversation. And it was, kind of, but it actually continued beyond that.

I listen to the recording. Joe is saying, "Ever since we started, I see you better and better. Because it takes time for people to really get together, to click. The more I see you, the more I feel you. You understand?"

"I do," I told him. "I feel the same way."

"And there's nothing you can take away from me. There's nothing that can change that, because we've built very good feelings. And it's between you and I, just the two of us. Okay?"

That's when he said "I love you" and I responded with the same.

On the recording, I can almost hear myself trying to turn the weight of that phrase that we've just shared over and over, trying to parse what this kind of love means. I venture, "it's very... you know..."

"You're beautiful, is all I can tell you," Joe says.

I laugh. Then, "hmmm." No follow-up, but it's clear that there's an inner dialogue I haven't shared.

Joe's not having it. "What? Come on, what? Say it. I know what's in your mind."

"I don't know," I tell him, honestly. "This is very real, I can't say it any other way."

"I know what you're thinking. Do it. Say it."

"I'm not really sure, I'm just thinking that this is so much beyond... *this*..." I picture me sweeping my hand over both of us, pulling us together in this "this" that we happened into.

"*Do it*. Do it. And feel it. And don't be afraid, because that's the way it is. That's life. Am I right or wrong?"

I laughed. He was always right.

"Listen," he went on. "You can say anything you want to me. Anything. Because I feel whatever you feel. So you can feel totally free. Okay? That's the way I want you."

The equating of love with total freedom, my distinct discomfort when Joe pushed me to name what I was feeling, the way he turned this feeling into a verb, a call to action (*DO it*)—

that was the actual culmination of the conversation.

free•dom\ 1 : the quality or state of being free: as **a** : the quality or state of not being coerced or constrained by fate, necessity, or circumstances in one's choices or actions **b (1)** : the status of the will as an uncaused cause of human actions : the absence of antecedent causal determination of human decisions **(2)** : self-realization or spiritual self-fulfillment that is not incompatible with the existence of natural causes of the will-act : SELF-DETERMINATION **c (1)** : exemption or liberation from slavery, imprisonment, or restraint from the undue, arbitrary, or despotic power and control of another : LIBERTY, INDEPENDENCE **(2)** : the ability or capacity to act without undue hindrance or restraint **d** : the quality or state of being exempt or released **e** : GENEROSITY, LARGENESS, MAGNANIMITY **f (1)** : EASE, FACILITY **(2)** : the quality or state of running or operating smoothly and without impediment **g** : the quality of being frank, open, unreserved, or outspoken **h** : improper familiarity : undue social liberty : violation of the strict dictates of decorum or decency **i** : boldness or vigor of conception or execution **j** : unrestricted use **2** : RIGHT, PRIVILEGE, FRANCHISE : as **a** : the right of participating as a member or a citizen often conferred as a mark of honorary distinction upon one who is not a member or a citizen **b** : a right or liberty guaranteed by a constitution or fundamental law or granted by one in authority or assured by convention or popular sentiment **c** : the right or privilege of availing oneself of speech or of acting according to the dictates of conscience or utilizing, supporting, and acting according to one's own view of religion without undue restraints or within reasonably formulated and legally specified limits

¹love \ 1 a : the attraction, desire, or affection felt for a person who arouses delight or admiration or elicits tenderness, sympathetic interest, or benevolence **b:** an assurance of love **2 a** : warm attachment, enthusiasm, or devotion (as to a pursuit or a concrete or ideal object) **b** : the object of such attachment or devotion **3 a** : the benevolence attributed to God as resembling a father's affection for his children **b** : men's adoration of God in gratitude or devotion

****

Freedom and love aren't exactly antagonistic terms, but they're not exactly intuitively connected either. Stealing liberally from Sartre, it's fair to say that freedom has two basic modes: *freedom from* and *freedom to*. In the first case, freedom is defined mainly in terms of negation or exemption or liberation. In the second, it's identified as a possession, right, or privilege implying a code of conduct. But what I'm noticing is that *freedom from,* as the entry implies, has its limits. The boundaries are, in fact, well-marked. And there can be judgment in the stepping-out of these boundaries: "improper familiarity," "undue social liberty" (see h, i, and j). This kind of freedom has the potential to disrupt, discount, relationships. On the other hand, *freedom to* reasserts the primacy of relation: rights or privileges bind the holder all the more tightly to the force that outlines and defines these rights and privileges.

Freedom to is charge and obligation.

It is attachment.

It is love.

When Joe pushed me in that moment to name our relationship (*Say it*), when he attached an implied code of action to my "saying it" (*Do it, and don't be afraid*), it felt so familiar, so simultaneously empowering and imposing. That day in that glassed-in boardroom, nobody there but us except for the occasional passerby looking at us strangely, I felt like my dad was *back*. Fully reincarnated and making me uncomfortable with the intensity and stakes of the conversation. Part of the discomfort stems from the fact that there's tension with Joe's family—the kind of tension that I imagine this sort of storytelling often creates. There's danger in the telling of these stories, after all, in who gets to tell them, in what can be said, in what can be felt, in who gets to feel. The existence of that tension, the feeling of being torn, the guilt that I'm creating conflict—that is a familiar space for me.

But there's more.

Joe's follow-up comment that I am "totally free" with him echoes a line that cuts through the cumulative noise of the many letters my dad wrote to me when I was growing up: "You have always had the freedom to express yourself and to expect my understanding." When I put these statements next to each other, a couple things strike me. First, that Joe and my dad would even feel it necessary to tell me that—as far as *we* go—I am free, suggests to me that, for both of them, freedom is not a given, it's not the default category. It's an exception, a rarity, something to be cherished. Second, for them, my freedom depends upon my honesty. My willingness to tell them the truth is what makes me free.

The freedom that defines my relationships with Joe and my dad is not the first kind—*freedom from* (though it can be argued that they demonstrate this kind of freedom, independently and respectively, as swagger and chutzpah). It's that second kind of freedom they're granting me, and asking me to exercise. *Freedom to*: to say the things that I feel in my gut have to be said. To trust that, to say them, is the only way to honor these relationships.

****

I know I've been skirting around the edge of what some might call profound disrespect and others might call irredeemably delusional, the way I've begun equating these two men—the survivor and the one who squandered his life. I know the risks of comparing a doctored resume to a name change in the midst of genocide, of collapsing charm to a general trait without distinguishing between the ways it was used, of likening chutzpah to swagger.

I know all that.

But I also know this: *when I'm in Joe's presence, my father is back*. He is. And I'm still trying to figure out what to do with that. The same wicked sense of humor, the same calling out of bullshit, the same cutting through to the heart of things, the same ability to see and call attention to the specialness of a moment that might pass unnoticed to others. In all the ways that mean the most to me, they are... the same.

There's that moment that changed everything in our relationship, that moment when Joe said we are the same because we both lost our fathers too soon. I have been wrestling ever since with what it means that Joe said that. With what it means for the way I have been telling Joe's story. With what it means, in general, for how stories like his can be told. With what it means that, on some level, beneath the heart-stopping grace I felt in that moment that Joe placed us together, I must have also heard, or wanted to hear, the opening up of possibility that this man holds a place in my heart that only my father had held before.

LAST THINGS

I still don't know what it was that convinced me to take on the project of working with Joe. When I look back, it seems both counter to my nature and entirely obvious. On a conscious level, I suppose I thought this would help me to re-energize, a mid-career project that would re-connect me to my work. Maybe I was thinking it would be a way to earn legitimacy or credibility, an embodied investment in a subject that had only been theoretical before. Maybe I thought it was a chance to redeem all of those ways that I had failed to be an actual scholar of the Holo-caust in my own eyes: an actual scholar would have gone through the camps, would have gone through the exhibit at the Holocaust Museum in Washington, I told myself. An actual scholar would have overcome her irrational rejection of these places and approached them with a critical and objective eye. Maybe I thought that working with a Holo-caust survivor could substitute for, could perhaps trump, all of those activities that felt like voyeurism to me.

At the end of the day, though, none of those conscious motivations, if these *were* the motivations, seem to matter much. They remain the dry stuff of academia, a way of keeping Joe at arm's length. What mat-ters is that I found my way to Joe. In my theory of convergence, it's need that swerves two paths together. People looking for each other, even if they don't consciously know they're looking. Consciously, I didn't know I was looking for Joe, and any academic motivations could have been fulfilled without him. It's the unconscious stuff, the wishes bound up with having lost my father too soon, that swerved my path towards Joe *specifically*.

Specificity matters in convergence, it's at the heart of the thing, it's how it operates. Predicated though it was on general labels—Joe: sur-vivor, Beth: scholar—my initial encounter with Joe only really became convergence once those labels fell apart. When I look back on it now, it seems to me that Joe resisted the label "survivor" from the start, and, so, for him, the falling apart was effortless. For him, it's always been about the afterlife of survival, the way he lives in the midst of a story still being told. Maybe that's why he was sometimes so reluctant to tell his own story. For me, where the story—The Suit—ended was an aesthetic choice. For Joe, there is no end, except for the end.

If it was easy for Joe to let go of labels and categories, then I clung to them. And that clinging-to was an imposition of my will where it shouldn't have been. The thing about convergence is that it happens when ego drops out of the mix. Convergence is letting-go. I've understood this equation on an intellectual level for quite some time, but I needed Joe to *feel* what letting-go means. I needed Joe to help me get over my own ego.

But, still, the question lingers as to *how* that letting go functions, or should function, or can function, in the context of telling a Holocaust story. And still, at the end as in the beginning, it's the representational piece that I wrestle with and against: *how* to tell this story? What are the obligations of *this kind* of storytelling? In her exquisite novel, *The History of Love*, Nicole Krauss gestures to the *how* that resonates most deeply with me. Her novel is a tone poem to *beshert* and to the insufficiencies of language to capture its contours. As with *Night*, a kind of silence embeds the narrative, the white space of the page asserting itself as the novel nears its end. "We couldn't use [the words of our childhood] in the same way and so we chose not to use them at all. Life demanded a new language," the main character, Leo Gursky—a Holocaust survivor—explains.[33] In Leo's explanation, I hear the enigmatic prescription that Paul Celan—also a Holocaust survivor—announces in his poem, "Sprich Auch Du" ("Speak, You Also"):

Speak, you also
Speak as the last one,
Have your say.

Speak—
But leave Yes and No unsplit.
Give your speech also this meaning
Give it its shadows.[34]

Years ago I parsed the words of this poem, looking for answers. Looking for the right questions. Now, on the other side of trying to tell

Joe's story, it makes a visceral sense to me: now it seems to me that the *how of telling* this kind of story—of memory and unbearable cruelty, of trauma and the rupturing of so much that is human, of the stark clarity of loss and its residual ache—has to be something like this. It has to enlist shadow, ambiguity, blurring-of-boundaries between No and Yes. It has to fracture, shatter, unravel in the telling. "He speaks true who speaks the shadows," Celan continues. A call to arms: the only kind of truth worth speaking is that which is coaxed from darkness, wrapped in language that, he writes, has had to "come through the thousand darknesses of murderous speech."[35] As with Krauss, Celan's "new language" reaches across this darkness, clasps hands and pulls towards, in a gesture of clumsy intimacy, raw, unscripted, real.

Now I understand.

Life demands this kind of language.

****

Back in that townhouse in Chicago, now so many years ago, when I first met Joe, I was fixed on the idea that he was a philosopher. It was a reductive and simplistic way to think about him, but there's still something in that original casting that remains compelling for me. It's not really the term itself that I'm tied to—there's not a trace of the inapplicable or ethereal or theoretical in the way Joe approaches his world. Everything Joe ever said to me is grounded in his own experience, and, because of this, it can't be systematized or fixed in stone or easily charted out. To the extent, though, that his experience forms the blueprint for his actions, that he thinks deliberately about the path he's taken and he wants others to learn something from his choices, it's fair to say that there is a philosophical component to the way he approaches the world.

But that's still pretty thin.

Here's what I think it is: I think what I'm trying to retrieve from that original desire to label Joe a philosopher is that, for me, the things Joe says have weight and importance and substance and meaning. They have implications and consequences. They matter to me in the same way that the words of so many of my literary and philosophical heroes have mattered. And my coming to realize that Joe sits next to these heroes has made them matter to me all the more. Joe has re-animated these heroes for me, saved them from the sterile world to which I somehow thought they (and I) were condemned. I imagine Joe alongside of those literary and philosophical giants, wagging his finger at Sylvia, trading jokes with Kafka, sparring linguistically with Nietzsche, now master of ceremonies, now life of the party.

As this picture takes shape in my mind, I'm reminded of a line from a letter Flaubert wrote, I think it was to Louise Colet, or maybe it was George Sand, that has always stuck with me. He relates a trip he's taken to the beach with his sister and her family. He describes a moment where he's sitting by himself on the sand, watching them play together in the waves. A voyeur, apart and alone. "They are in the real," he thinks to himself, deeply melancholy, coming to the awareness that his own life lacks the intimacy and fulfillment he's just witnessed. *"They are in the real."* Kafka quotes this line in his diaries, with the same heartbreaking self-awareness. And all of a sudden I realize that, in all the ways that matter most to me, Joe has in fact surpassed many of my heroes. For all of their brilliance, for all of the ways they have shaped the way I see the world, these heroes did not live lives that I would have chosen. They shut themselves off from others, held people at arm's length, protected their hearts and thoughts and visions at the expense of losing the "real." I hear Joe shouting at would-be dwellers and *kvetchers*—"you're here, you're alive, you've got love, you've got a family... what the hell is going on?!" I hear him announcing his values—life, love, family—and it occurs to me that Joe is more an existentialist, more a yes-sayer than any of the writers whose words I've so long admired on the page.

I see now that it was the swagger spilling out from the pages of those early drafts that drew me to Joe and kept me chasing a story that swelled beyond its own boundaries. Any standard dictionary definition equates swagger with arrogance or over-confidence, but that's never what I've meant when I've used the term to describe Joe. For me, it's context specific: it has to do with the reverence and hushed whispers with which we too often greet the term Holocaust, with the way so much Holocaust remembrance encourages us to walk on eggshells. Joe's swagger is his defiance of this posture, the way he insists that everything is fair game and nothing is off limits. The way he defines his own terms and offers up entirely new ways of thinking. The way he refuses to dwell, instead looking at the world as a problem that he can solve. The way he sees possibility where others see only obstacles.

Joe's swagger has made it clearer to me why I bristle at the mantra so often associated with Holocaust memorials—"never forget." Before Joe, I couldn't really articulate what it was about this phrase that felt off, beyond the fact that it felt narrow, or bitter, or resentful. These were judgments that I had no business assigning. Now, in Joe's presence, I hear "never forget" as getting stuck, as dwelling. It's a claustrophobic phrase, and it keeps us walking on those eggshells, afraid to speak. In an aesthetic sense, as I've wrestled with how to tell Joe's story, the mantra now seems to me to lend itself to formulas and clichés, as if the precise language and ways we are called on to preserve memory have already been determined for us. In this sense, "never forget" feels scripted, generic: hard-to-hear speeches on far-away podiums. "Never forget" encourages monologue, solitary voices uninterrupted by chance encounter.

Joe has helped me to understand why "always remember" makes more sense to me, both in terms of Holocaust memorializing and memory-making in general. Always remembering is dialogue, and all the messiness that comes with it: digressions, circlings-back, bubblings-up, interruptions, stammers and false starts. It is necessarily cruder and less manageable than never forgetting. But it is also so much more intimate, so much more authentic, so much more active. Always remembering is unprecedented, unmediated, unreserved, expansive, innovative. Always remembering is swagger.

Joe said to me once:

"I hate the Germans for one reason: because they took everything I had in my life, the most dearest people in my life. I will never, ever, ever forgive them for that, as long as I live.... We have to live now, but you can never forget it, deep down in your heart, you remember what they do to you and you never, ever forgive them for that. I know what I got. I know what I feel."

When I look at this statement now, I zero in on the self-awareness of the line, "I know what I feel." I was wrong to read what sometimes seemed like Joe's desire to move on in our conversations as resistance to reflection. I've come to realize that he moves with his memories in the space of reflection, in constant dialogue with his past, shaping an ever more knowable sense of himself. "I know what I feel" is a declaration of strength: Joe knows who he is, he knows where he came from, and he knows in his heart where his memories can and cannot take him. There is no getting through or getting over but *we have to live now*. This is how Joe remembers, how he lives now.

As much as his swagger, it's also Joe's kindness—his empathy—that I keep coming back to. The way he was so quick to forgive the glaring holes in my knowledge and experience, my narrow sense that book learning could stand in for true understanding. The way he invited me into his life and made space for me in the midst of us trying to nail down his story. The way he never diminished my pain. "Everybody has their *pekl*," he insisted, drawing us closer, encouraging me to say anything and everything. The way he affirmed my own sense of worlds converging precisely when they needed to.

Joe has taught me that convergence happens in the space of living now, in the space of always remembering, in the space where swagger and vulnerability paradoxically come together. After all, those simple and child-like wishes that led me to Joe—to be seen, to be heard, to be understood, to feel something other than alone—are vulnerable and precarious. They are wishes that can only be asked of and granted by others. Joe met my vulnerability and answered it with his own. "You feel the same way?" he asked me. "You do? You feel the same?"

****

The last time I saw Joe, I didn't know it would be the last time. I would have hugged him tighter had I known. It was that day in the Corner Bakery, when I wrestled with his son and wife over whether or not to include the word "shit" in the story I was crafting for them. The dispute seems petty now, even if the stakes behind it—to get Joe's story right, to capture him as accurately as possible—remain high.

We talked on the phone a few times after that day, and I sent him the manuscript I'd written, with a long accompanying letter describing how much he had come to mean to me, how grateful I was for his presence in my life. Over the years, I sent the occasional Chanukah card and holiday family picture. I think I once sent cookies. But we'd lost something in the larger disputes over who had rights to the material— also petty in the grand scheme of things—that ensued once Joe's family had The Suit. As he did that day in the Corner Bakery, Joe looked on, amused, at the silliness of it all, rising above us. I tried to protect him, as I'm sure his family did, from the acrimony that was building. But things got a little ugly, and time got away from us.

Missing Joe, I would play the recordings over and over, needing to hear his voice, his laugh. And the tattered couch in Brunswick, Maine, where I spent my sabbatical recollecting my thoughts and reassessing my materials in another attempt to get Joe's story right, with its holes in the cushions and foam padding peeking out, became a kind of refuge. A place where I could sit with Joe again at that table in the glassed-in boardroom on Wacker Drive, Lake Michigan spreading out behind us.

There was one moment in particular that I kept coming back to, solace and confirmation of what had taken place between us, even as it all felt like it was slipping away. It was the last minute of that 36-minute conversation we'd had, the one about my not-going to see the camps, when he'd told me he loved me.

Once, in reliving this moment, I was overcome with how much I missed him. I picked up the glossy paperback containing The Suit that sat always next to me on the couch as I worked. Looked at Joe's wide grin on the back cover. Locked eyes with him. I snapped my computer shut and jumped up from the couch. This time I wasn't nervous. I didn't have to work up my courage. I ran to the phone and called Joe.

His wife answered. She was a little taken aback by my calling out of the blue, but thoroughly gracious and kind. She told me that she had recently had to put him in a home, that he was struggling with dementia. That he knew what was happening to him, but couldn't communicate.

"You know, it's funny," she said, "the way life works... the Holocaust was a horrible, horrible thing for Joe when it happened. It ripped his life apart. But, in the end of his life, it's the thing that's saving him. He goes to the Museum once a week, and he sits there and hands out books, and his caregiver talks for him. People are funny... it's like they just want to be able to see him to know that what happened, happened."

A blow—to learn that he was once again locked in the prison of his own mind, unable to tell people his story in his own words.

But I hear his insistent, "if I want to cry, I cry to myself, because the only one who really cares about it is me. You got it? *No one will ever really understand how I feel*. To lose a family—the only one who can do it, the only one who can know is the one who goes through it. So I just act how I act and know what I know and that's it. Am I right?"

And I hope it gives him some comfort to have become the living symbol of this standing-apart and alone.

"Can I write to him," I asked her. "Can I talk to him?" Trying—and failing—to contain my sobs. Thoughtless, to have put her through this. My call out of the blue, my inability to hold back tears. Her having to comfort me when her own pain must be unbearable.

"No," she said, "he won't be able to read what you write. But you can send a card and some pictures and I can read it to him. He'd like that."

I did. That day I found a card that said "forever in my heart" on the front. I placed two pictures inside—one of my husband, my boys, and me at a recent wedding, all dressed up, the other of my boys and me cuddled together on top of a mountain.

I told him how much I miss him, how I carry him with me all the time, how I'm still working to find a way to tell his story that will do honor to him, how I can't wait to show it to him.

And signed it, "All my love."

NOTES

1 *Subverting Scriptures: Critical Reflections on the Use of the Bible.* Palgrave Macmillan, 2009.

2 Technically, I was never officially "hired," in that I never signed a written contract or acceptedmoney from the family.

3 He did, later that day. There were two. The first draft, titled "Recollecting My Life," was written "with" Sari Steinberg, over the course of two years, 2005-2007. The second was written "with" I.K Hoffman in January, 2008, titled "I Choose Life." The "with" in the author attribution made clear, and the drafts bore out, that these women were charged with transcribing Joe's story.

4 *Reluctant Theologians: Franz Kafka, Paul Celan, Edmond Jabès.* Fordham University Press, 2002.

5 Somewhere in the midst of my writing, the details are fuzzy, let's say early spring 2009, I managed to track down Sari (couldn't find I.K.). I wanted to make sure it was all right with her that I had and was using her draft. It was. It was clear, though, that things hadn't gone so well between her and the family, and that she loved and missed Joe deeply.

6 For more information, see https://sfi.usc.edu/vha/collecting

7 "There Are Just 100,000 Holocaust Survivors Alive Today," Time. July 3, 2016. time.com/4392413/elie-wiesel-holocaust-survivors-remaining/

8 ibid.

9 My note to Joe:

July 29, 2009

Dear Joe,

Hi! Hope all is well! Here's the draft, at long last.

I wanted to explain a few things about the choices I made, because it's probably not exactly what you were expecting. And of course we can talk about all of this, but I thought it might be helpful for you to hear why I took the approach that I did.

So, here goes...

My imagined audience in writing this is a general audience, interested in these sorts of issues, who care about what it means to try to capture a story like yours. In my view, and I don't mean to sound mean or anything, there are too many Holocaust memoirs that create a caricature of their subject. You are not a caricature; you are a living, breathing, three-dimensional person with a life of your own. And there's no simple way to capture you and what you have gone through. Many memoirs of this sort fall back on clichés or kitsch; they, therefore, become somewhat sentimental and don't ask anything of the reader. But there are big, philosophical questions surrounding what it means to tell your story, and how we should tell it. I want our readers to at least consider these questions, even if there's no easy way to answer them.

My audience, then, is not necessarily your family, or at least, not only your family. I certainly hope that they see you reflected in all of your glory here, and that they feel I have captured you faithfully. Primarily, though, I am hoping to introduce you to the world beyond your family. The world is going to love you!

The most important thing to me in writing this is to capture you and your voice for our readers. You have such wonderful and original and funny and wise things to say, and I want our readers to hear these things in your own voice. To me, your voice comes through most powerfully when you are talking about your experiences, when you describe later how you've come to view them. So, what I've tried to do here is interweave the "action" scenes themselves (of your experience during the war) with our discussions about these scenes and the sorts of issues that are raised. What is so important about telling your story is not only to let people know that it happened (this is extremely important), but to make people think about what it means to live in a world in which this could have happened. You have things to say about this—incredibly moving things—and I want readers to think about your reflections as an integral part of the story itself.

Over the course of our meetings, we have developed a beautiful relationship. I cannot describe to you how important you have become to me, how my meeting you at precisely the moment that I met you seems almost magical to me. I'm not a religious person, but there feels like some kind of fate in my meeting you. Our relationship, it seems to me, is also an important part of the story. Readers will be wondering what the heck I'm doing here, and why I'm the one telling this story. So, I decided to weave a little bit of this into the mix as well. Not too much, I hope, but enough so that readers can see how much you mean to me and why. I also want readers to see how differently we think about things, and how narrow my "academic" viewpoint really is. I want them to see you forcing me to change my mind—to reconsider some of my narrow viewpoints. There will be many different ways of looking at the world represented by our readers, but I've tried to put us into dialogue with one another (with you getting the last word) when it seems important to show the range of approaches to various issues.

The question of where to begin and where to end was something that I wrestled with a lot in writing this. I decided to begin your story with the circumstances that force you to hide in Gestapo headquarters and to end with your experience in the Israeli army. I know that this leaves out A LOT, and I hope that you don't feel that I am diminishing the importance of your life before and after these moments. What I thought we could do, to provide readers with a fuller understanding of your life before and after, is to include a pretty extensive section of pictures at the end—of your life before the war, with your family, and then after, perhaps of you in Israel, and then when you come to the US. I'd like to include recent pictures, too, of you with your family, and perhaps one last picture of the two of us. I also plan to include at the end of the book an annotated timeline that would allow me to show the movement of war through Czestochowa, and a map to situate readers. If we include all of these things, I really feel that readers will have a full picture of you and who you are, and will have quick access to some of the details that don't come up in the narrative itself. My goal in writing was to keep things moving as quickly as possible, to keep readers interested—to get in and get out quickly, as it were. I think we'll do best with this approach, because we will give readers something that they can read and digest rather easily, but still leave them with a host of larger questions to contemplate at the end.

Okay, guess I should stop explaining and just let you get to reading. I hope you know—and hope it comes across—how very grateful and honored I am to be writing this. I think you are a most remarkable person, and only hope that I have been able to do justice to you and your story.

Much love,

Beth

10 *Diaries of Franz Kafka.* Trans. Hannah Arendt, Joseph Kresh, Martin Greenberg. New York: Schocken Books, 1975, 222.

11 There is a chapter detailing this part of Joe's life in the manuscript the family self-published. In the version I gave to the family, I named the chapter "In Israel." The family renamed the chapter "The Holy Land," a choice that feels to me a particularly far departure from my own sense of the project. I chose not to include this section in Part One because it never felt well-written to me; it felt, instead, belabored and artificial. My own political commitments could never accommodate the title "holy land" as a way of describing Israel, and I chafe at the theological overtones bound up in "redeeming" Joe's Holocaust experience through his emigration to Israel.

12 This is the approach Sari Steinberg and I.K. Hoffman use in their drafts.

13 *The Things They Carried.* Houghton Mifflin, 1990, 71.

14 *Survival in Auschwitz.* Touchstone Edition, 1996, 9.

15 *Night.* Bantam Books, 1960, 32.

16 *Man's Search for Meaning*, Beacon Press Edition, 2006, 13.

17 *The Things They Carried*, 68-69.

18 In the version of the manuscript they printed and sold at the Holocaust Museum in Skokie, the family changed the line to "'Oh no,' he thought. 'This was bad.'"

19 *The Things They Carried*, 77.

20 My deepest thanks to John K. Roth, Edward J. Sexton Professor Emeritus of Philosophy and

Founding Director, The Center for the Study of the Holocaust, Genocide, and Human Rights

Claremont McKenna College, my friend and mentor, for providing this analogy during one of our many conversations about how I might approach the telling of Joe's story.

21 *Tough Jews: Fathers, Sons and Gangster Dreams.* Vintage, 1999.

22 *The Avengers: A Jewish War Story.* Vintage, 2001.

23 In *Ariel.* HarperPerennial, 1961.

24 *Survival in Auschwitz*, 22.

25 *Morality After Auschwitz: The Radical Challenge of the Nazi Ethic.* Fortress Press, 1988, 2.

26 I'm actually pretty obsessed with the thesis of this book, which inspired me to write the essay, "Morality After Auschwitz?: Haas, Nietzsche and the possibilities for revaluation" for a collection of essays— *The Double Binds of Ethics After the Holocaust: Salvaging the Fragments.* Palgrave Macmillan, 2009—compiled by the participants of a seminar I attended at The Center for Advanced Holocaust Studies in July 2001. The seminar was entitled: "Ethics After the Holocaust: Key Issues in Philosophy and Religion."

27 I don't have a copy of this newsletter. See here for more information on the society: http://www.czestochowajews.org/eng_jews.htm

28 *Survival in Auschwitz*, 13.

29 *Angel at the Fence: The True Story of a Love that Survived.* The book was scheduled to be published by Berkley Books in 2009, but was ultimately never published.

30 See http://www.cnn.com/2008/US/12/30/holocaust.hoax.love.

story/

31 See http://forward.com/opinion/14846/a-danger-greater-than-de-nial-03080/

32 *Denying the Holocaust: The Growing Assault on Truth and Memory.* Plume, 1994.

33 *The History of Love.* W.W Norton and Co., 2005.

34 *Poems of Paul Celan.* Trans. Michael Hamburger. New York: Persea Books, 1972.

I adapted the translation.

35 "Speech on the Occasion of Receiving the Literature Prize of the Free Hanseatic City of Bremen," *Paul Celan: Collected Prose.* Trans. Rosmarie Waldrop. New York: Sheep Meadow Press, 1986.

ACKNOWLEDGMENTS

Just as convergence—*beshert*—is a central motif in this book, it is also the energy that has swirled around the book's making, from beginning to end. It has been a long and winding path, shaped by so many forces. With tremendous gratitude and an overwhelming sense of meant-to-be, I would like to acknowledge this collective shaping.

First and foremost, my profound thanks to Joe's family for giving me the chance to listen to and tell Joe's story. And to Joe, for whom thanks seem not-nearly-enough: *you have changed my life.*

To Sari Steinberg and I.K Hoffman, whose drafts of Joe's story of survival provided a blueprint for our conversations and details that were tremendously useful for the crafting of the "Suit."

To John Roth, dear friend, teacher, mentor, inspiration: you are the lens through which I first confronted and continue to confront the Holocaust, and through which I attempt to process these confrontations. Your support and encouragement for this project have meant the world to me. *Thank you.*

To Hank Greenspan, whose seminal book, *On Listening to Holocaust Survivors*, looms over each page of *Ghost Writer* as conscious and subconscious charge to listen actively and to hear deeply. And to David Harris-Gershon, whose courageous and exquisite memoir, *What Do You Buy the Children of the Terrorist who Tried to Kill Your Wife?*, looms just as fully as template for breaking the rules of storytelling.

To the generous readers who met and helped to craft this story along the way: Lynn Price, Tom Chiarella, Sarah Gerkensmeyer, Josh Goldberg, Bill Little, Johnny Bartlett. Each in your own way, you have been guides and seers, prodding the story in directions it wanted to take.

To Chloe Walker and Elias Altman: you were and are meant-to-be part of the story of this book, which bears such deep traces of your dedication.

To Shem Rees, soul brother, whose illustrations grace the front and back cover: thank you for conjuring images that so perfectly capture the core of this story, but still manage to leave the core ineffable.

To the editors at Spuyten Duyvil, especially Aurelia Lavallee and Tod Thilleman, for their gracious and loving reception and preparation of this story and book. To Spuyten Duyvil, with these extraordinary people who care intensely about the nurturing power of the written word, *Ghost Writer* has found its way home.

Finally, but most importantly, to my husband, Jim, and my sons, Cam and Tobey: my reason for being, without you there would be no wish to tell this story or any other.

BETH BENEDIX is a Professor of World Literature, Religious Studies, and Community Engagement at DePauw University. She is the author of *Reluctant Theologians: Franz Kafka, Paul Celan, Edmond Jabès* (Fordham University Press, 2003), editor of and contributor to *Subverting Scriptures: Critical Reflections on the Use of the Bible* (Palgrave Macmillan, 2009), and a contributor of chapters, articles, introductions and reviews to a variety of collections and journals. She is Founder and Director of The Castle (www.castlearts.org), a non-profit organization that provides integrated-arts and project-based workshops in Putnam County, Indiana, public schools. Beth lives in Greencastle, IN with her husband and two sons.

CPSIA information can be obtained
at www.ICGtesting.com
Printed in the USA
BVHW04s0612020518
514456BV00058B/58/P